"In today's crowded and noisy marketplace, humanity wins. Maria Ross's compelling book shows—through research, case studies, and practical advice—how compassion and cultivating an empathetic mindset can help leaders and brands stand out."

DORIE CLARK author of *Stand Out* and *Reinventing You* and
adjunct professor at Duke University's Fuqua School of Business

"Today, the products and services of Company A and Company B are often engineered and optimized until they are indistinguishable. But one differentiator remains: empathy. This is a wise, passionate, motivating book that's a must-read for every manager and executive."

JAY BAER founder of Convince & Convert
and coauthor of *Talk Triggers*

"Maria Ross shares hard-won lessons about the power of empathy from her experiences in the healthcare system and her years as a brand strategist to some of the top brands in the world to empower leaders and businesses of all kinds to treat their stakeholders with the compassion and care required to build customers for life. She provides practical steps for any organization to shift their cultural mindset in ways that will not only increase their productivity, retention, and financial success, but also improve their personal interactions. This book is exactly what we need right now to ensure our world is a lot more livable for all of us."

DENISE BROSSEAU CEO of Thought Leadership Lab and
bestselling author of *Ready to Be a Thought Leader?*

"Relationships are critical to success and your greatest asset. To enable productive relationships with colleagues, subordinates, and customers, individuals must approach those connections with empathy and compassion. This book brings theory and action together in one powerful resource to help organizations create a connected culture and prioritize people to fuel success. Empathy is a concept that needs to be embraced in the workplace—and Maria Ross shows us exactly how to do it."

MICHELLE TILLIS LEDERMAN author of *The Connector's Advantage* and *The 11 Laws of Likability*

"Maria Ross is the perfect person to impart this wisdom because she's an enthusiastic brand builder and her personal journey has been about giving and receiving life-affirming compassion. Not only does her book share insights about how empathetic leaders can drive outsized impact for their businesses, she engages the reader with her witty and heartwarming storytelling. This is one of those rare business books that is not just informative, but optimistic and enjoyable."

MEGAN HANLEY CMO of Freedom Financial

"Maria Ross brings practical, compelling insights to one of the key attributes we must all build and grow if we hope to thrive on this planet: empathy. Empathy is one of those roots that will ground your success in all aspects of your life. The ability to understand others' perspectives gives us a design edge for our business, an understanding of differences that creates more powerful relationships, and a happiness factor that is priceless. Read this book if you want to level up in all parts of your life."

VICKI SAUNDERS founder of SheEO and #radicalgenerosity

"Today, when top talent seeks not just a paycheck, but purpose and fulfillment at work, Maria Ross shows us that empathy is the foundation of thriving careers and cultures. Those organizations that figure it out will be the ones that succeed in the new economy, and those that don't will be increasingly irrelevant—losing talent, productivity, and market demand. This book goes beyond theory to lay out specific actions leaders can take to build the brands and cultures of the future."

AARON HURST cofounder and CEO of Imperative
and bestselling author of *The Purpose Economy*

"The workplace is now more diverse than ever before. Building a stronger culture starts by relating to each other, regardless of background, age, or life experience. Maria Ross shows that empathy can be your superpower if you want to achieve your goals. She gives you solid tips to help you build your emotional intelligence, and harness the power of diverse perspectives if you want your organization to thrive."

CHIP CONLEY hospitality entrepreneur
and *New York Times*-bestselling author

"Maria Ross's insightful book couldn't have come at a better time. She shows why empathy is an intangible good that customers will happily pay for. *The Empathy Edge* is a wave worth riding."

MARTY NEUMEIER author of *The Brand Gap*

"The best marketers are able to articulate 'the compelling reason to purchase' their products and services. Maria Ross has crystallized this idea and given it a voice—today, empathy is the lens through which marketers can best understand what motivates their customer to choose their products over the competition."

GUY WEISMANTEL CMO of Pushpay

THE EMPATHY EDGE

Harnessing the Value of Compassion as an Engine for Success

A playbook for brands, leaders, and teams

MARIA ROSS

PAGE TWO
BOOKS

Cataloguing in publication information is available from Library and Archives Canada.

ISBN 978-1-989025-79-6 (paperback)
ISBN 978-1-989025-80-2 (ebook)

Page Two
www.pagetwo.com

Edited by Amanda Lewis
Cover and interior design by Setareh Ashrafologhalai
Printed and bound in Canada by Friesens
Distributed in Canada by Raincoast Books
Distributed in the US and internationally by Publishers Group West, a division of Ingram

19 20 21 22 23   5 4 3 2 1

www.red-slice.com
www.theempathyedge.com
#EmpathyEdge

Every reasonable effort has been made to contact the copyright holders for work reproduced in this book.

Also by Maria Ross

Branding Basics for Small Business: How to Create an Irresistible Brand on Any Budget (2nd Edition)

Rebooting My Brain: How a Freak Aneurysm Reframed My Life

The Juicy Guides for entrepreneurs (mini-ebook series):

The Juicy Guide to Entrepreneurship: Advice on How to Energize Your Brand and Squeeze More Soul into Your Business

The Juicy Guide to Brand Building: Advice on How to Attract Loyal Fans and Amplify Your Message

The Juicy Guide to Time Management and Goal Setting: Advice on How to Wrangle Your Calendar and Slay Overwhelm

The Juicy Guide to Entrepreneurial Inspiration: Advice on How to Spark Your Creativity and Activate Your Inner Fire

CONTENTS

For Callum,

*here is my small but mighty attempt to make
the world a better place for you, my love*

If there is any one secret of success, it lies in the ability to get the other person's point of view and see things from that person's angle as well as your own.

HENRY FORD

INTRODUCTION
Empathy at Work

I HAVE ALWAYS BELIEVED that compassion, empathy, and kindness can be big assets in the business world. Throughout my career, I sought to rewrite the prevailing cultural script about business success: one *could* be compassionately competitive, kindly ambitious, and empathetic yet decisive. This mindset resulted in great success for me personally, as well as for my employers and clients.

I also believe that companies can make money *while* acting with kindness and empathy. The two are not mutually exclusive.

My understanding of the importance of empathy in business became much more personal in August 2008 when I awoke in a hospital ICU. My head was half-shaved and I had IVs in my arm. I was unable to see and had no short-term memory.

A few days earlier, I had been suffering from an intense headache and vomiting—symptoms that had plagued me for almost two months but, on that particular day, had left me unable to function. My husband had decided to leave work at midday, so, luckily, he was home when I'd collapsed, unconscious, on our bathroom floor. At the age of thirty-five—in the healthy, vibrant prime of my life—I'd experienced a ruptured brain aneurysm. An ambulance rushed me to the hospital, where emergency surgery saved my life.

I was in the hospital for six weeks, first in the neurological ICU and then in-patient rehab. The slow work of recovery began. The cerebral rupture was so severe that it caused hemorrhaging in my retinas, resulting in near blindness. Surgery in my left eye and more than ten months of recovery for my right eye eventually reversed the damage.

That time is mostly lost to me, save for a few snatches of memory here and there, like images remembered from a dream. Temporarily without my short-term memory, I didn't become fully aware of my surroundings until September, even though I was awake and talking to people.

Harborview Medical Center and the University of Washington Medical Center (UWMC), both part of UW Medicine in Seattle, was where I began the long process of reclaiming my life. Not only did the "brain ninjas" pull me back from the brink, but the care and compassion I received as a patient deeply impacted me. When you're sick or injured, you are extraordinarily vulnerable. You lie in a bed, weak and sometimes half-dressed, while doctors and nurses come in at all hours to poke and prod you. Medical students observe you like you are some sort of oddity. You are left alone and helpless for long stretches with nothing but a TV and a call button. You feel exposed and totally reliant on strangers.

Sadly, many healthcare systems are structured in ways that leave patients feeling insignificant and burdensome at a time when empathy is needed most acutely. But UWMC, like many hospitals around the world, believes in and practices Patient and Family Centered Care (PFCC).

PFCC is a global movement that recognizes the importance of patient input and family (or caregiver) involvement in ensuring positive recovery outcomes. It's a framework for honoring the unique skills, strengths, and preferences of each patient so their input becomes integral to medical decisions throughout the process. The core pillars of PFCC include information sharing, collaboration, and respect.

In other words, hospitals using PFCC are putting policies, processes, and resources in place that focus on their patients' needs and feelings, essentially treating them like, you know, *humans*, not assets or beds. These hospitals are seeing better health outcomes, improved quality of care, improved safety, higher satisfaction ratings, reduced hospitalization and re-admission rates, better clinical and staff satisfaction, and a wiser allocation of resources. All those benefits translate to reduced costs, higher profits, and positive goodwill for the organization and its brand.

UWMC, like many other hospitals focused on PFCC, has adopted empathy as their watchword to better serve patients, resulting in better patient outcomes, improved internal morale, and, yes, some damn good press.

When I awoke, scared and confused and unable to remember anything from one moment to the next, my family and I knew nothing about PFCC. But during this vulnerable time in the hospital, here's what we observed:

- No one—be they doctor, administrator, or nurse—ever walked into my room without first knocking, introducing themselves (to this temporarily blind woman), and asking if they could come in.

- My husband was able to be by my side for as long as I needed him. There were no official visiting hours.

- Any time instructions were given, hospital staff ensured I had my caregiver (or a proxy) in the room to take notes since I could not remember or sometimes even process the conversation. If they had to wait for someone to be there, they would.

- My dignity and intelligence were honored when staff took the time to explain recommended procedures, jargon, or acronyms as well as answer any questions we had.

- When I asked for help as I stumbled through the hallway with my impaired sight, or my family needed assistance, no one ever said, "That's not my job." They always stopped what they were doing and found the right person to help us.

- I was given the power to choose my food every day from a menu of options. This small semblance of control during a scary crisis meant so much to me—and it also meant I had a lot of chocolate cream pie.

- The hospital helped coordinate my post-discharge care and followed up with numerous phone calls and check-ins. They even gave us a binder of resources and contact numbers should we have any questions.

The experience was so profound that when I fully recovered, I began volunteering for UWMC's patient and family education committee as a patient advisor. By doing so, I was able to represent the voice of patients as the staff made key decisions.

Imagine: an organization that treats its "customers" not in the ways employees themselves would like to be treated but the way the *individual customer* wants to be treated. An organization whose business model has been set up to gain efficiencies, decrease costs, and increase customer satisfaction based on compassion and taking another person's point of view.

That's the power of empathy at work.

ALTHOUGH THIS TRANSFORMATIVE experience kicked my own compassion into high gear, I've been a student of empathy all my life. I identify as a storyteller, and empathy is core to this lifelong passion of mine. I know from experience that stories have the power to inspire, provoke, teach, delight, and motivate us. And in order to tell a good story, you must be able to use empathy to live in someone else's world, understand their point of view, and imagine their emotions and experiences. The empathy that drives storytelling is at the heart of my work as a brand strategist, helping companies articulate and share their value to connect more fully with their customers, clients, or constituents.

We are experiencing, as former president Barack Obama so eloquently put it, an "empathy deficit." He was referring to the United States, but I think we can extend this lack of empathy to the whole planet. Too many people are taking sides, ostracizing the "other," and generally failing to be on their best behavior. We've become numb to tragedy, we accept the hurtful comments of Internet trolls as standard behavior, and we hide behind screens rather than connect with those around us on buses, in playgrounds, and at coffee shops. Many sense this chasm but are not sure how to cross it. Some feel empathetic but are left wringing their hands and not knowing how to put that empathy into compassionate action.

What better way to chip away at this dilemma than by starting with the place where a lot of us spend more than forty hours each week: work.

If organizational leaders can shift the cultural mindset around what gives a business a competitive advantage and show how empathy can increase financial success, productivity, and retention (among other benefits we'll explore in this book), maybe the positive behaviors individuals adopt as a result will spill over into their personal interactions. Maybe, just maybe, our world could become a little bit better. A sneaky access point, I know. But logical and, as we'll see in these pages, extremely possible.

While I'm a brand strategist and not an empathy scientist, I've found that sometimes an outsider with deep and persistent curiosity can serve as a helpful guide through a subject; in fact, sometimes it takes this fresh perspective to see the nuances of the big picture and bring everything into focus. As a bonus, when you don't know "the rules" inherent to a particular topic, you're not afraid to break them. (Or gleefully stomp them to smithereens, when necessary.) You can explore in innovative ways, ask taboo questions without hesitation, and tease out unexpected conclusions.

I am an expert in how empathy plays a key role in effective, resonant brand strategy. I've been crafting brand blueprints and marketing strategies for more than twenty-five years. My clients range from Fortune 500 companies to fast-growth startups to scrappy solopreneurs. *All* of them want to appear accessible and compassionate in their brand messaging and connect with their customers, yet they don't always know how to support that desire with authentic action. I help them make those connections and walk their empathetic talk. Together, we ferret out how they can highlight their empathetic strengths so their customers or clients believe their brand claims. And as an extension, we often end up talking about how effective leaders seem to get inside their customers' heads (and, in turn, the heads of another key audience: their employees) to achieve better engagement. Our conversation about branding leads to one about how to change hiring practices, internal policies, or customer service processes to truly *be* an empathetic brand.

I've done countless hours of consulting around what empathy really means to organizations. I've shown them how to live it every day, instead of just slapping some appealingly compassionate language on their websites. Connecting empathy to work is something I do constantly and naturally. In this book, I'll share how you can use some of the same empathy practices I employ to help clients connect to their customers as a way of strengthening your leadership style, deepening your workplace culture, and building a brand of which you and your colleagues can feel proud.

Because, let's face it, there's never been a better time to break the outdated rules of how business *should* work and build a truly empathetic company.

Organizations now have an unprecedented opportunity to transform their cultures, for better or worse. There are three main reasons:

1. For-profit companies are reshaping their role in society.
2. Employees are working more hours but also have more options about where to work.
3. Technological changes sweeping into organizations are changing our roles, and those changes require our uniquely human skills to be effective.

Let's look at how powerful for-profit organizations are redefining their roles. In the 1980s, corporate America adopted economist Milton Friedman's view, as summarized by the *Seattle Times*, that "a company's sole social responsibility is to make money for its owners without breaking the law." But many organizations are now wielding their considerable clout to do more good in the world, a concept known as *conscious capitalism*.

Several years ago, Howard Schultz, former CEO and now chairman emeritus of Starbucks, made it his mission to take a stand on political, societal, and often controversial topics, such as race relations, veteran affairs, and LGBTQ rights. In an interview quoted in the *Seattle Times* in 2015, Schultz said, "The size and the scale of the company and the platform that we have allows us, I think, to project a voice into the debate, and hopefully that's for good... We are leading [Starbucks] to try to redefine the role and responsibility of a public company."

And even companies who don't yet have compassion built into their mission statements have stepped up to voice their collective concerns over social injustices. When things got ugly during the 2016 U.S. presidential election, many were heartened to see corporations using their power to defy the closed-minded, sexist, and xenophobic rhetoric being tossed about. While many individuals felt powerless, influential organizations were able to take a bold and effective stand on racial equality, immigrant acceptance, and LGBTQ and women's rights. And many of them did so using one of the largest platforms of all: 2017's Super Bowl broadcast.

Advertiser 84 Lumber chose to depict a Mexican mother and daughter trying to seek asylum in the United States, where they are heartbroken to find that—after all their journey's struggles and obstacles—they are met by a large wall. The commercial concluded as a hopeful cliffhanger, with the young girl pulling out collected scraps that formed an American flag; online, viewers got to see a happy ending where the pair eventually find a door, built with 84 Lumber, of course.

In another Super Bowl ad, Audi presented a charming story of a concerned father whose little girl competes against all the boys in a soapbox derby. The dad relays his fears that "she will never be seen as—or paid at a rate—equal to men." But in the end, he wants to rewrite the story for her, and the ad speaks to the company's commitment to equal pay.

While there were calls for boycotts because of such ads, there were many more people who showed support, vowing to shop with these companies and reward them with their dollars.

With simple television spots, these for-profit companies showed us that they could indeed make an empathetic impact and, in some cases, transform the culture and conversation. They could show us the best of ourselves and encourage us to be decent human beings, all while promoting their own products and boosting their bottom lines. If they embraced empathy as a core value and earnestly lived it out, they might be able to create an example and help to establish a new norm of compassion among us all.

Another reason that organizations are poised to change the conversation around empathy is that employees are working longer and harder than they have in the past—and they are more willing to leave a position if they are unhappy. The average American, for example, works close to fifty hours per week and those who are able will leave a job if they believe the company is mistreating them or their customers. Notwithstanding the negative psychological and health impacts that more hours at work can have, this is a wake-up call to organizations to transform *the way* they work before it's too late. People are seeking ways to make their long work hours more fulfilling, and this is much easier to do when they work for a company that aligns with their own values and treats them with respect.

Enter empathy.

While in-demand talent spends slightly more time at work, they now also have more options. They won't tolerate working in environments that do not respect them as workers or value their customers. If they sense a manager or a company in general is not understanding, values-driven, or able to treat their customers right, they are happy to job hop.

Rebecca Friese Rodskog, cofounder and managing partner of FutureLeaderNow, advises companies on how to create more innovative workplaces and cultures so employees can thrive, which trickles down into reduced turnover, more productivity, and amazing brand experiences for customers. She has pointed out that if organizations want to attract the best talent and keep them happy, it's imperative that they nurture leaders, create cultures, and build brands that align with their workforce's core values. If your organization can't identify employee core values, you'll fail to attract and retain great people. If your company crafts a mission statement that has no place for worker input or runs counter to employee beliefs, that mission will crash and burn. If your leadership is embarrassingly out of touch with life among the ranks, they'll never inspire innovation and creativity in their employee base.

So, how do you understand their perspectives, listen to their needs, and identify their core values? How do you ensure your organization engages, rewards, and supports its workers?

In a word, empathy.

In an age when algorithms and robots seem to be taking over the business landscape, it would be easy to assume a "soft skill" like empathy would no longer be needed. Nothing could be further from the truth.

Heed the words of tech futurist Christina "CK" Kerley, who advises some of the world's largest companies on how to embrace, not fear, the technological changes that are coming our way. From her vantage point, it is imperative that leaders and organizations start talking empathy. Given all this automation, these so-called soft skills will matter most. The very qualities that make us uniquely *human* will become our competitive advantage. Robots won't render us obsolete: instead they will make our human skills more relevant than ever.

SOME OF YOU might see empathy as a savvy PR move that will earn your company more customer loyalty... and dollars. And it's true that building an empathetic brand means more customer loyalty, which translates to more revenue.

Believe it or not, I'm glad you're reading this book, too.

I once worked as a marketing manager for a global company. Among other duties, I helped clients who were facing strong competition for the first time create positive brand perceptions. These clients would often partner with community organizations to support charitable events, school programs, and populations in need. I tried to steer clients toward the more charitable, high-impact efforts that would showcase them as good corporate citizens. For a mere $5,000, I told them, we could donate an entire semi-trailer full of food to a local food bank. Our clients were good people who loved the idea of filling the shelves for hungry people (who wouldn't?), but at the end of the day, they were doing it for good press. The media would show up, hands would be shaken, photos snapped, and the clients would look like a bunch of damned heroes. In my mind, we were still doing a good thing—even if the client was doing it for selfish reasons. After all, at the end of the day, the food bank would be stocked and hungry people could eat. Until the big day arrived, and I saw how it all went down.

Executive bigwigs showed up alongside excited frontline employees. They were there to help unload the truck and pound the backs of the food bank volunteers—but also for the photo ops. They'd planned on the great PR, but they didn't plan on being genuinely moved by seeing how much good their generous gift would do and how many lives they'd impact. They didn't plan on making real connections with the volunteers and patrons, taking on individual volunteer shifts after the event, or forging an ongoing relationship with the charity. They didn't plan on having their empathy stirred. But it was. And they were transformed, right on the spot.

If you do a good deed for a selfish reason, are you a scoundrel? Maybe. If you see visibly empathetic business practices as a great way to add some shine to your company reputation, are you an opportunist? Perhaps. But the pragmatist is willing to accept the value in impactful deeds even if they stem from underhanded motivations. After all, you can have all the internal empathy in the known universe, but if you don't act upon it, you'll never spark change outside yourself. Forcing yourself to go through the motions of acting compassionately can cause genuine compassion to take root.

Naturally, I'd love for everyone who reads this book to embrace compassionate tactics because they are supportive and sustainable. But those of you who are here for that shiny topcoat of empathy that you believe will boost your bottom line? You are welcome, too. I will Trojan horse you into authentic empathy if I have to.

I want all of us to understand empathy's role in our daily lives and, more importantly, how we can turn our heartfelt *feelings* into positive *actions*. I want every person within an organization, at every level, to see that empathy is an asset, not a weakness. I am recruiting you to my Empathetic Army as someone who enthusiastically spreads the word that authentic connection breeds phenomenal success. While empathy currently offers an edge in the market because it is so rare, the traits and practices shared in this book will (hopefully) soon become the organizational standard.

To be authentic and sustainable, we must practice empathy from the inside out. It starts with leaders adopting an empathetic mindset and leadership style. This, in turn, influences the internal culture that they create. And, finally, that way of being informs the everyday actions of those people on their customers and the community, thus creating an empathetic brand impression and reputation.

The book is broken out in sections to discuss how each circle builds on the next, creating a ripple effect.

Here's what I hope you will take away from reading this book:

- a belief that empathy is an asset for entrepreneurs and organizations;

- proof that active empathy fuels great businesses and brands and creates profitable, scalable infrastructures;

- habits and practices that will help you become a more empathetic leader and create thriving cultures where your teams stay loyal and can do their best work;

- policies that your organization can adopt to create a positive and empathetic brand reputation with your customers, community,... and future hires;

- tangible actions to cultivate empathy and have an impact right where you are and *right now*, regardless of the size of your sphere of influence; and

- a desire to spread the word that authentic connection breeds success.

I want to live in a world where empathy forms the backbone of all business. A world in which we align our personal and professional values, so we don't have to be two different people at home and at work.

And I need your help building it.

How? Let's look at how empathy shows up in successful companies of all sizes, not just charitable organizations or non-profits. Read on to learn how the best and most progressive leaders and businesses have begun to adopt and employ mindfully compassionate business tactics—and what you can do to put these into practice in your own work and organization.

So, let's get started.

PART I

WHY MORE BUSINESSES NEED TO CULTIVATE EMPATHY NOW

1

EMPATHY EXPLORED

Empathy isn't dictated to us by a focus group or a statistical analysis. Empathy is the powerful (and rare) ability to imagine what motivates someone else to act.

SETH GODIN

CHRISTINA HARBRIDGE WAS an eighteen-year-old college student when her dad became very ill. Determined to support him through his sickness, she searched for a way to make money, take care of him, and continue going to school. She began working part-time at a collection agency. The work was emotionally taxing but paid double minimum wage and allowed her to juggle her other responsibilities. It was far from perfect, but she knew it would have to do.

On her first day at work, Harbridge met her new colleagues. They were some of the nicest people she had ever met, and as they gathered together in the break room, she thought maybe the job wouldn't be so bad after all. But when they returned to the collection floor and everyone began making calls, Harbridge could not believe her ears. She stood at a filing cabinet, unable to breathe, her hands shaking. The colleagues who had been so friendly and jovial toward each other were cruel and awful toward the people from whom the agency was trying to collect payments. They yelled, they shamed, they used scare tactics freely and without remorse. She was appalled by this night-and-day switch.

"I was pretty young and I was like, 'What the hell is this?'" says Harbridge. "I saw in that moment—I literally remember what I was wearing, it was so profound—I thought, *Somebody's got to start a collection agency that works by being nice.* We were making and taking thousands of phone calls. What if these phone calls actually made people's days?"

She couldn't get the idea out of her head.

While Harbridge worked her agency job, she kept trying to change company policies and customer service tactics from the inside as best she could, but it was no use. She later switched gears and started writing software for collection agencies. But the spark of that first-day idea remained, and eventually she started her own agency, building it around the idea that kindness could go hand in hand with collections.

"I had no idea what I was doing," Harbridge says, "but I knew we were going to make this work by being nice. Maybe we won't collect as much, but people will *want* to work with us."

She keenly recognized that collection agents are usually the last type of contact a company attempts when a customer owes them money. And because many of Harbridge's agency's clients were healthcare providers, she and her employees were calling patients—vulnerable people who were ill or in pain. She knew the healthcare providers would want courteous, respectful people to be making those connections on their behalf. Harbridge was convinced there was a market for companies outside the healthcare industry who wanted their collection customers to be treated well, too. She believed that the number-one goal of a collection call was not to get money right away: it was to establish a trusting relationship, so people felt comfortable telling you the truth. "If they tell you what's going on, you can help them," Harbridge says. "A lot of the calls the industry was making were about getting compliance rather than building trust and commitment."

Harbridge's collection agency broke the rules. For thirty minutes each day, her team met in a circle and did various exercises to help them "stay in love with people." This training was designed to help her employees stay open and empathetic during a tough day spent in conversation with people who are deeply upset. Harbridge was not fooling herself: these are not fun calls to get, nor are they enjoyable calls to make. And she estimates that more than 70 percent of the people on the other end of the line were, understandably, distraught and rattled when her employees explained why they were calling.

"Our biology doesn't want to give empathy when we're uncomfortable," says Harbridge. Instead, she says, "We want to correct people." In other words, being nice when someone is yelling at you requires a lot of human development and careful system design. She created the daily training practice to bolster her people's confidence and remind them that they were doing good and important work—the calls needed to be made, but they were making them in the most empathetic way possible.

This approach paid off. "There was a direct correlation between how the debtor felt about themselves when we called them and whether or not they paid," says Harbridge. Her agency ended up collecting three times more than the industry average: 32.2 percent successful collections as opposed to the typical 9.9 percent. In addition, her collectors did such a fabulous job of establishing trusting, supportive relationships with their clients that they regularly received thank-you cards, even wedding invitations!

"I am not kidding about that," she says, laughing. "We also had to have a toy box in the front of our office because so many people brought their kids to meet their bill collectors."

To what does Harbridge attribute her collection agency's success? Quite frankly, she stumbled upon the power of empathy at work simply because she believed it was the right thing to do. Instead of just telling her people to "be nicer," Harbridge led by example. She changed processes and developed training to support the behaviors she wanted to see, and she established an internal culture that helped her collectors thrive. As a leader, she provided needed and consistent support each day to her team. She even created a bonus structure that didn't simply reward employees for the amount of money collected alone, but instead tallied up the number of thank-you cards they received. (Unsolicited cards, of course. Team members weren't allowed to request a thank-you card from a client.) And guess what? The person with the most money collected usually had the most thank-you cards, too.

Harbridge believes that the reason debtors not only paid up but also invited her team to their weddings is because her company's leadership, culture, and external brand reputation were all rooted in empathy. The trust they built was genuine; they were trained to earnestly care about the people they were contacting.

"We gave them a feeling they weren't getting anywhere else, which was 'I hear you, I understand you, and I want to know more. Tell me more.' When someone was upset, we weren't faux-listening; we were fulfilling their need to be heard and understood."

The most telling revelation: her team members' total surprise at how effective this kindness-focused approach could be. Seasoned collection agents were shocked by how much easier their jobs became when they acted with empathy instead of shaming, degrading, and disrespecting debtors.

"It was accidental, the revenue success," says Harbridge. "We did it because we thought there was a market for people wanting their customers to be treated well. It really transformed my thinking about humans."

Many organizations reached out to Harbridge, trying to figure out how she did what she did. Even politicians wanted to understand her secret sauce and sought her advice. Harbridge eventually founded Allegory, a behavior change consultancy that helps companies and leaders achieve higher performance by fostering more emotional literacy with and between employees and customers. This means helping teams work with uncomfortable internal and external situations and emotions, so they can be okay with not being okay. Allegory sees "discomfort as delicious" and believes that when teams allow discomfort, they can improve outcomes. Allegory's goal is to teach companies to create a productive environment where real feelings are expressed, people are heard, and each situation is approached in a way that turns feedback into productive action.

"Feelings drive behavior," Harbridge says. "If someone makes us feel small, we're probably not going to buy from them—or work hard for them, if they are the boss. That may induce compliance but not commitment. Any organization that is missing empathy with customers is missing sales, and any leader lacking empathy is missing opportunities to be more successful. Not a very rational strategy."

Harbridge's success is a powerful example of what empathy can do when infused into the fabric of an organization at every level. She broke the mold in her industry by insisting that the work could and *should* be done with empathy at its heart, and she proved that her revolutionary approach could lead to phenomenal success.

What about those of us who feel ready to incorporate more empathy into our own work but aren't sure where to start? How do entrepreneurs launching startups *and* employees of established global corporations enact change? How can we flex our empathy muscles to benefit not only ourselves but also the organizations for which we work and, ultimately, our customers? What can companies gain from fostering empathy at the leadership, internal culture, and external brand levels? How can that success transform the players and, in the process, make us all better humans?

To answer these questions, we need to examine what empathy is, how it influences our behavior, and what we can do to cultivate and deploy it in our working lives. We also need to understand where empathy comes from, so we can foster it in ourselves and others.

What Is Empathy?

You probably have an idea of what empathy is or isn't, at least according to your own experience. But before we dig any deeper into how empathy develops and impacts our lives, we need to get on the same page as to what empathy *means*. Is empathy the same as sympathy or compassion?

The word *sympathy*, which stems from the Greek *sympatheia*, or "fellow-feeling," back in the mid-1500s meant something akin to being in harmony with someone. But today, "it tends to convey commiseration, pity, or feelings of sorrow for someone else who is experiencing misfortune." *Empathy*, introduced centuries later, is what we feel when we haven't necessarily had the same experience but can actively imagine what that experience might have felt like, and perhaps (but not necessarily) even feel some of their emotions ourselves. It's about putting ourselves in the shoes of another.

Parissa Behnia, executive coach, business consultant, and creator of the Sixense Empathy Model™, illustrates the difference, saying, "Empathy worries about the drivers to how someone got to a point in time. Sympathy is me standing directly in front of someone and just judging only what I see in front of me. Sympathy does not care about the steps someone took to get to that point in time—it only cares about the outcome in the moment. Empathy understands the outcome and how you got there."

You don't have to have personal experience with a specific set of circumstances to have empathy. You just need to understand and respect the steps taken along that journey.

Next, let's clear up how empathy differs from compassion. The words are often used interchangeably, and they reference related concepts, but they're not exact synonyms.

Empathy is a perception, urge, or mindset. It has to do with putting yourself in someone else's place and imagining what life is like for them.

Compassion, to me, is activity, decision making, or response. It has to do with *taking action* that results in kindness, typically toward another person or group.

Such action can be fueled by either empathy or sympathy, says Sara Schairer, founder and CEO of Compassion It, a global movement to encourage daily acts of compassion, and a Stanford-trained teacher of Compassion Cultivation Training (CCT). She writes, "Compassion takes empathy and sympathy a step further. When you are compassionate, you feel the pain of another (i.e., empathy) or you recognize that the person is in pain (i.e., sympathy), and then you do your best to alleviate the person's suffering from that situation."

I think of empathy as the engine but compassion as the result, or the expression of empathy. Compassion doesn't always stem from empathy. It can, but it doesn't have to.

Think about a middle-income office worker walking past a homeless woman who asks for a dollar. The office worker gives the woman the dollar, which can be seen as a compassionate act: help was asked for and given. Dig deeper, and that dollar could have been given out of empathy: the office worker could have a family member who was or is homeless, be a veteran and know former military personnel homelessness is on the rise, or simply be able to imagine how stressful it would be to have no home. In that case, giving the dollar is a compassionate act driven by empathy. But the office worker might feel guilty about the other dozen times he passed this homeless woman and didn't offer help or feel pity, or he was impatient to get on with his day and sees giving the dollar as a quick fix. In that case, he is acting compassionately without even *attempting* to put himself in the homeless woman's shoes.

Susan Spinrad Esterly has been a psychologist for more than twenty years. She used to be a professor at the Institute of Transpersonal Psychology, which was one of the few schools in the world that espoused humanistic values such as mindfulness, empathy, and compassion before they became fashionable and prevalent in leadership circles.

"Empathy essentially asks you to have an idea of what someone else is experiencing, seeing, sensing," she says. "Compassion, I think, is broader than empathy because compassion says, 'I will put love in there with it.'" Esterly goes on to say that without that good intent, empathy can have a dark, manipulative side. "The best con artists are probably, oddly, very empathic in terms of getting where someone else is coming from and using that to motivate them."

Even disentangled from compassion, empathy is a contentious concept. The various definitions can divide people as decisively as a sports debate between Yankee and Red Sox fans. Scientists and scholars continually argue about what empathy really is, its relevance to modern life, and its function within societies, bringing some fascinating conundrums to light. Let's examine a few of these expert opinions before defining the function of empathy for the purposes of this book.

Psychologist Paul Bloom, author of the controversial book *Against Empathy*, defines empathy as "the act of coming to experience the world as you think someone else does. If your suffering makes me suffer, if I feel what you feel, that's empathy." He believes that acting on purely emotional empathy is myopic, short-sighted, and unsustainable. He argues that emotional empathy can sometimes impair our ability to make rational decisions in certain situations or think clearly about the long-term consequences of those actions on others.

To illustrate, he cites a study done by C. Daniel Batson and his colleagues, in which subjects were told about a ten-year-old girl named Sheri Summers, a child with a fatal disease who is in line for a treatment that would alleviate her pain. When subjects were simply asked what to do, they fairly decided that she needed to wait her turn on the list because more needy children were ahead of her. When they were asked to imagine what she *felt*, however, they tended to move her up on the list, putting her ahead of other children who needed the treatment more.

Bloom states, "Empathy is like a spotlight directing attention and aid to where it's needed. But spotlights have a narrow focus, and this is one problem with empathy. It does poorly in a world where there are many people in need and where the effects of one's actions are diffuse, often delayed, and difficult to compute, a world in which an act that helps one person in the here and now can lead to greater suffering in the future."

I should note that Bloom and his contemporaries are not against *compassion*. They're not heartless human beings. They make the case that there is more to kindness and morality than empathy alone, and that both the pros and cons should be considered. Bloom advises against making all decisions based solely on emotional empathy—in essence, based on a feeling—because that can lead to ignoring or denouncing logic, facts, or science, something which is happening in our world today far too often.

On the other hand, many classical thinkers and modern thought leaders believe empathy in all its forms is essential to human survival and to making the world a better place. Charles Darwin—though most well known for *On the Origin of Species* and the concept of survival of the fittest—strongly made a case that cooperation and reciprocity were as vital to evolutionary success as competition. In *The Descent of Man*, Darwin wrote, "Those communities which included the greatest number of the most sympathetic members would flourish best and rear the greatest number of offspring." It should be noted that he used the term *sympathy* to mean our modern definition of *empathy*.

In fact, sympathy and empathy were used interchangeably before Darwin came on the scene. Social scientist Roman Krznaric writes in his book *Empathy: Why It Matters, and How to Get It*, that early references to empathy evoked the sentiment but did not use the actual word. While eighteenth-century Scottish social thinker Adam Smith championed self-interest as the catalyst for societal improvement in *The Wealth of Nations*—and is often seen as a forefather to the "Greed is right. Greed works" business philosophy menacingly portrayed in the film *Wall Street*—he surprisingly started defining empathy in his earlier work, *The Theory of Moral Sentiments*. Smith used the term *sympathy* but, according to Krznaric, "argued that we have a natural capacity for stepping into another person's shoes," which Smith described as "changing places in fancy with the sufferer."

In short, people have been arguing about these definitions, distinctions, and semantics for hundreds of years. No wonder empathy has become such a heated and confusing topic!

But let's fast-forward to the twenty-first century, shall we? There's still plenty of disagreement in the present day, but it emerges more subtly. In recent years, prominent figures in politics, science, business, and art have examined empathy's modern meaning and underlined its importance within contemporary culture. For instance, in a college commencement speech, Barack Obama urged graduates "to see the world through the eyes of those who are different from us— the child who's hungry, the steelworker who's been laid off, the family who lost the entire life they built together when the storm came to town. When you think like this—when you choose to broaden your ambit of concern and empathize with the plight of others, whether they are close friends or distant strangers—it becomes harder not to act, harder not to help."

Author and leadership expert Simon Sinek shares this sentiment and emphasizes that empathy is crucial to successful leadership. He defines empathy as "the ability to recognize and share other people's feelings," and he believes it's "the most important instrument in a leader's toolbox."

So, although a subset of experts assert that empathy has risks and negative repercussions, many respected scientists and leaders from diverse backgrounds believe that empathy isn't just beneficial, it's *vital*. Still, those thinkers may be using wildly different definitions of the word. In fact, every person I interviewed for this book had a slightly different interpretation of what empathy meant to them and what it meant in an organizational context. However, some common themes did emerge in their responses. Empathy means:

- seeing things through another person's perspective;

- crossing a line of difference to experience someone else's truth and reality;

- having enough understanding and sensitivity toward a situation, scenario, or person to try to make that situation, scenario, or person better than it would be if you lacked that understanding;

- the ability to sit with discomfort and not have to fix it;

- listening and hearing what is going on for someone else; and

- moving through the world with an understanding that everyone is struggling and trying their best—and holding that in your heart to let it shape your interactions with people.

Common threads—including understanding outside perspectives and a desire to connect—weave through these varied interpretations. The nuances are diverse, but concepts of respect, sensitivity, and shared feelings unite them.

What's that? All this talk about feelings is making you roll your eyes? Fear not. There are two huge reasons to embrace empathetic tactics in your business life.

First, social psychology distinguishes between two types of empathy. *Emotional empathy* means you feel how the other person feels, full stop. This is what many of us think of when we think of empathy. You literally experience their fears, anger, anxieties, and excitement as if they were all happening to you. Studies of mirror neurons have shown that this emotional empathy is an instinctive trait in human beings and other animals. But *cognitive empathy* means you understand how another person sees the world. This is the type of empathy that Bloom and his contemporaries have no issues with and are comfortable accepting.

Such perspective-taking can then intellectually inform your reaction in the situation—often solving the problem with compassion. Being empathetic doesn't negate your ability to make a rational, reasoned business decision.

Second, emotional connection, stories, and experiences drive current business trends. A 2017 Forbes.com article states, "In today's age of brand experience, it seems that emotional engagement is proving to be more and more critical to achieving winning results, and effective storytelling and digital marketing are at the heart of this movement." Empathy can play a big role in creating that emotional engagement.

The importance of empathy to business success plays out in the work of Fierce Conversations, a Seattle-based company that works with clients to have tough, honest, and richer conversations so they can clarify priorities, reduce costs, and boost profits. Its philosophy is that many of the organizational problems that manifest as high turnover, low productivity, or missed goals stem from ineffective conversations. And the root of effective conversations is often—you guessed it— more empathy and a greater ability to take perspective.

Fierce has seen incredible results for clients that tackle operational challenges from a training and communications perspective. "Our work used to be, and can still to some current extent be, classified as soft skills," says president Stacey Engle. "The reality is that conversation skills are *hard skills*. What gets talked about, how it gets talked about, and who gets invited to the table determines what will happen... or won't happen... We must answer questions like, 'What are the real business pain points your team is experiencing?' and be willing to listen to their point of view. The missed deadlines, the losing sales, the constant rework, and on and on—those absolutely are tied to empathetic communication... and those have real top- and bottom-line impacts."

For this book, let's agree to examine empathy through this lens:

Empathy means being willing and able to see, understand, and (where appropriate) feel another person's perspective and, further, to use that information to act compassionately.

The action part is key: how are individual behaviors, internal practices, or external dealings informed by an empathetic mindset? It's not enough to *feel* or even *claim* empathy; people and organizations need to *act* on it.

Action. This is the fundamental link that many definitions of empathy miss. Empathy drives compassionate action, and such action is what can drive business success.

Dr. Zanette Johnson agrees. She is an experience designer, management consultant, neuroscientist, and mindfulness practitioner who earned her PhD at Stanford in learning science and technology design. "A lot of the definitions of empathy seem fundamentally incomplete to me because they are thought-oriented and neglect the body, as well as the experience of action," she explains. "To me, compassion is empathy in action."

Let's be very clear: being an empathetic organization does not mean caving to demands or simply "giving the employee/customer/colleague what they want." That's not empathy; that's submission. Empathy is more of a mindset that guides the interaction and ultimate action or policy, rather than blind acquiescence.

Being an empathetic organization also does not mean accepting a weak place in the market. Yes, you can be empathetic *and* competitive. In fact, companies that keep empathy top of mind are capable of building more robust brands than those who ignore it. Quality messaging is imbued with empathy. It projects the impression that the entity selling goods or services thoroughly understands your emotions, needs, and desires as a consumer. Empathy-focused brands are capable of forging strong, lasting relationships with their customers; relationships that translate into hard dollars and strong results, as we saw through the story of Christina Harbridge's compassionate collection agency.

Better Than Gold: The Platinum Rule

We often think of empathy as the Golden Rule: *do unto others as you would have done unto you.* That's compassionate, right? But here's the problem: not everyone thinks or feels the way you do. We all come at situations with different experiences, baggage, and perspectives. Treating others how we'd like to be treated means assuming our own preferences are universal. Not a good plan.

Belinda Parmar—founder and CEO of The Empathy Business and creator of the Global Empathy Index—sums this up beautifully: "If you treat others like *you* want to be treated, your frame of reference is yourself."

A better way to act with empathy is to follow what has become known as the Platinum Rule: *Treat others as they want to be treated.* Flipping the old version of this rule forces you to see things from the other person's point of view and *then* choose the right course of action—the definition of empathy we're talking about here.

In *Drive: The Surprising Truth about What Motivates Us,* Daniel H. Pink shatters the old myths about the best ways to spark stellar performance. While one-size-fits-all "carrot and stick" approaches made work more efficient decades ago, the complexities of modern economies and required skills of the current century require new motivators. Great thinkers like Abraham Maslow questioned the assumption that all humans respond to stimuli in the same way. Pink cites research and case studies throughout *Drive* that support this, showing how motivators differ for different types of people, and that the same rewards—for example, increased pay—do not always motivate everyone in the same way. In some surprising instances, providing financial rewards can actually backfire. For intrinsically motivated, creative thinkers, autonomy, mastery, and purpose are far more effective motivators, which can have startling productivity and business benefits when employed in the right way.

Empathy Overwhelm

There's a human tendency to think that if we can't help everyone or create a big enough dent in the problem, we shouldn't even try. This is a counterproductive way to look at large-scale challenges, and one that experts deem a false sense of inefficacy, or *pseudo inefficacy*. It ignores the snowball effect of small actions and provides an easy excuse for shirking responsibility. Organizations can still do the right thing for a large portion of their employees and customers even if they can't help everyone.

Paul Slovic is a psychologist at the University of Oregon, and for decades he's been asking why the world often ignores mass suffering or atrocities. Slovic's work has shown that the human mind is not very good at thinking about, and empathizing with, millions or billions of individuals. His findings show that when the number is too large, we tend to dehumanize people and don't feel anything toward their specific situation, what Slovic calls *psychic numbing*.

I believe that this happens to many of us, either as entrepreneurs or as part of a larger organization. Business owners or sole proprietors (solopreneurs) can often feel that they have to "play the game" as it's written in order to succeed, leaving no room for empathy or human connection. Trying to change the way business gets done in their industry is too daunting of a task to take on, or they feel like their individual efforts as a small business owner won't cause seismic shifts in cultural business norms. That's why when we hear about renegades such as Richard Branson, Arianna Huffington, or Herb Kelleher of Southwest Airlines shattering business norms, it's incredibly inspiring. On the other end of the employment spectrum, people who are one of thousands of workers within a larger corporation often feel powerless to improve an entrenched culture that rewards cutthroat competition over collaboration or one in which they can't bring their whole selves to work for fear of being misunderstood. They see an immovable behemoth in front of them. It's a David versus Goliath situation, and the best course of self-preservation is often to leave rather than try to change the organization from within.

BUT THIS BOOK will hopefully give you the tools and practices to make change from wherever you stand. Changing our mindsets in business can spill over into the larger culture. You are going to meet some innovative companies and leaders in this book who are already doing this work and fighting this fight.

In Part II, I'll show you how leaders can adopt a more empathetic mindset to manage their workplaces and lead their teams in a way that engenders loyalty, productivity, and peak performance. We'll explore rituals and practices to help you strengthen your empathy muscles to get the best out of the people around you—even if you don't identify as a particularly empathetic person. Creating a workplace culture with established practices that reinforce empathetic action can actually make you more empathetic. Psychologist Susan Spinrad Esterly states from her experience working with patients,

"I can tell you that people who are autistic or on the spectrum and have difficulty with social cues can get a ton of help if they work on having rote lists of things that empathetic people do and try them out. Even if it isn't initially coming from a genuine place, the positive reinforcement is cyclical. Through time and positive reinforcement, the rote behaviors become ingrained and integrated." Basically, if you start doing the actions, this can lead to fundamental changes within you. She also says, "If people start changing what they do or if entities start changing what they do, they will start getting different feedback from the world."

In Part III, I'll describe empathetic workplace cultures to show you how companies can work from the inside out—on their culture and processes—to adopt and exhibit compassionate behaviors that, in turn, infuse the external brand. If you believe your organization could never, ever change its existing culture, consider this: organizational processes are made by humans and, therefore, can be changed and improved. Even a soft skill such as empathy can be codified and rewarded to encourage adoption, regardless of people's moods or emotional capacity. Slovic talks about this idea of creating processes and policies to account for human emotions, saying, "It's like the income tax system: we don't leave it to individuals' feelings of how much they think they should pay to the government for the services they receive... We don't leave it to people's feelings of loyalty and obligation; we couldn't. I think it's the same thing with these moral crises— when you think carefully and you realize the scale, you have to create laws and institutions that are not sensitive to the feelings of the moment."

Effective leadership and workplace culture come together to create fertile soil where people's innate empathy can take root. Creating this environment allows an organization's external brand to be believed as more empathetic. This crucial outward perception is what helps the organization differentiate, attract more customers, and inspire loyalty and referrals. In Part IV, we'll look at how to build an empathetic external brand and discuss the resulting benefits. We'll explore the various ways to embed empathy into the DNA of your organization so that it is authentic and real.

But first, let's dive into the ways that cultivating empathy within your own organization can help you grow and prosper.

Sharpen Your Empathy Edge

- *Empathy* is about putting yourself in someone else's shoes and understanding their emotional state because you have experienced something similar, or can imagine what life is like for them. It differs from *sympathy*, which is an acknowledgment of someone's emotional hardship, and *compassion*, which is empathy in action.
- *Emotional empathy* means you feel how the other person feels, full stop. *Cognitive empathy* means you understand how another person sees the world.
- Being empathetic doesn't negate your ability to make a rational, reasoned business decision.
- Being an empathetic organization or leader does not mean caving to demands. Empathy is a mindset that guides the interaction and ultimate action or policy, rather than blind acquiescence.
- Being an empathetic organization does not mean accepting a weak place in the market. Yes, you can be empathetic and competitive.
- In all dealings, endeavor to follow the Platinum Rule: treat others as *they* want to be treated.

2

THE BUSINESS
ADVANTAGES OF EMPATHY

Empathy as a way of understanding the world is underused.
JANE FULTON SURI, PARTNER EMERITUS AND
EXECUTIVE DESIGN DIRECTOR, IDEO

NOW WE GET to the heart of the matter: how is empathy good for business? Some say it is merely a "nice to have" trait, or something employees should strive for because it benefits the organization in terms of improved interpersonal relationships.

Au contraire.

Empathy has been shown to have a direct impact on everything from customer loyalty to innovation to profits. Let's explore each benefit in more detail.

Empathy Spurs Innovation

From the early 2000s to the mid 2010s, Microsoft was losing market share to Apple and other upstart competitors. The company was handsomely profitable in many areas, but its brand had grown stale. Windows Vista had been a huge flop and the company was late to the party on search technology (Bing) as well as social media. Microsoft had built its brand on innovation, but it was no longer seen as an innovative leader. While other tech companies had created disruptive technologies, taken advantage of digital culture, and effectively attracted the best talent to harness more creativity and innovation, Microsoft had become "the man"—a bureaucratic machine.

The internal culture reflected this. Many a Microsoft employee felt like a cog. I have colleagues and friends, including my husband, who worked for the company during these fallow years and suffered through a stifling culture full of confusing and constant change. Team and division reorganizations seemed to happen every six months, leading to changing roles and expectations that employees barely understood before the next major reshuffle. This shaky culture had an impact on Microsoft's ability to keep pace with changing market demands. The company offered definite opportunities and advantages as an employer, to be sure, but they had lost sight of what their customers wanted and, frankly, what their employees needed.

The good news is that the company realized this before it was too late. It began when Steve Ballmer left as CEO in 2014 and was replaced by Satya Nadella, Microsoft's third CEO in its history. A long-time company leader, Nadella's stints at Microsoft included serving as senior vice-president of research and development (R&D) for the online services division and as vice-president of the Microsoft business division. Nadella is often credited with transforming the company's business and technology culture from client services to cloud infrastructure and services, thus finally keeping pace with emerging technology trends. He is also credited with growing his business units by billions of dollars. Nadella has started turning the Microsoft ship around. And his primary leadership strategy? Empathy.

Nadella strongly believes that empathy is the driver of innovation. How can a company build future-forward products or services if it doesn't understand how a customer operates in their work and what they need to be successful? Especially if they can't yet articulate what they need because it doesn't exist yet.

Nadella understands that empathy is a powerful muscle for a leader to flex in order to better connect with customers as well as their own team. "In addition to confidence, a CEO must have empathy," Nadella told the Wharton School. It may be a quality one doesn't typically see on a list of top CEO character traits, but, as reported by the Wharton School, Nadella sees empathy as "a key source of business innovation. He said that although many regard it as a 'soft skill,' not especially relevant to the 'hard work of business,' it is a wellspring for innovation, since innovation comes from one's ability to grasp customers' unmet, unarticulated needs."

Let's pivot from Microsoft to the company that has been one of their strongest innovation challengers: Google. The company's founders, Larry Page and Sergey Brin, used to insist that only those with degrees in computer science or engineering could understand technology. Society's current emphasis on STEM skills (science, technology, engineering, and math) over softer skills or those based on emotional intelligence (such as empathy) seems to echo this philosophy. So Google decided to dig in to the data, as they are so good at doing, and see if this belief panned out.

It didn't.

The company released a study dubbed Project Aristotle in the spring of 2017 that underlined how important soft skills are, even in high-tech environments. The project examined data from Google's most "inventive and productive teams" to discover what made them so effective. The company has long trumpeted its top-notch people, killer teams, and ability to churn out innovative ideas on a regular basis but had implied that all of these things were due to technical skill and overall intelligence. Project Aristotle revealed that Google's "most important and productive new ideas come from B-teams comprised of employees who don't always have to be the smartest people in the room."

And if empathy can fuel innovation at these two mega-companies, just imagine what it can do for yours.

Empathy Aligns You with Customer Wants and Needs

When you encourage empathy among your workforce and parlay that mindset outward to customers, your company will thrive. Why? Because empathetic businesses better understand their customers and can anticipate their wants and needs—delivering solutions to the market that customers crave. The more in tune with your customers you can be, the faster you can deliver such products or services to them before your competitors catch on.

In my work helping businesses craft strong, successful brands, the most powerful exercise is creating ideal customer profiles. Not generic proclamations such as "We serve women between the ages of twenty-five and sixty" but an actual, detailed sketch of a person. Someone with a name, age, family life, interests, and more. I instruct them to make this person as real as possible, based on research, past customers, and their own common sense. What makes this person tick? What is their life like? What do they fear, value, crave, or worry about? It is only through completing this type of exercise that a company can see the world through its customer's eyes and understand what drives buying behaviors. The more empathy one can muster when crafting this profile, the more useful it can be to the business. Empathy can help leaders determine the right pricing, features, packaging, and even content and messaging that will most appeal to this person. And it will help them figure out the best way to promote the offering and get in front of this customer.

This process of empathizing with the consumer goes beyond sending out annual surveys or providing an email address for customers to "send their thoughts." It's about creating such a close relationship with your customers that you can immediately create solutions for their challenges.

Airbnb is a great example. The home-sharing site considers the property owners, or "hosts," part of their family and their customer base. If it cannot keep the homeowners happy, it will have no product to sell. Early on in the company's history, some of the hosts lost thousands of dollars when renters trashed their residences. The hosts not only had to deal with damaged property but also manage repair-related headaches and lost income opportunities while the home was being fixed. The company empathized with both those affected as well as those who now might fear renting out their properties and began offering a $50,000 insurance policy, which has since expanded into a $1 million policy.

Apple has also modeled the importance of empathy in understanding customer needs. Ellen Petry Leanse is a leadership consultant and author who teaches a course at Stanford University about the neuroscience of creativity and innovation, but she got her start at Apple. Early in her career, she was in product management during Steve Jobs's tenure and the company's rise in the '80s and '90s. During that time, she helped run global product introductions and, as Apple's first user evangelist in the mid-'80s, she launched Apple's first online connection to global users, helping customers share feedback on Apple products and what they needed from the company. While such user forums are commonplace now, since consumers can simply reach out to a brand via social media, this type of interaction and customer influence was revolutionary in a pre-Internet, pre-email time. While working at Apple, Leanse learned firsthand about empathy in action: understanding what your customer wants to *feel*.

"A critical lesson I learned at Apple, and from Steve Jobs, was that the product is not the product," Leanse says. "It is a delivery vehicle for a change in the lives, emotions, or hearts of the person you wish to serve with that product. Design the change and then you'll back into the product."

In order to know what customers desire, we must see things from their perspective: empathize with them. Most people only make decisions to add things to their lives when those things fulfill a specific vision for themselves. Leanse feels this is empathy as competitive advantage.

"My feeling is that Steve had a unique form of empathy—one people don't often understand," says Leanse. "He genuinely believed that everyone had more potential and desire than conventional norms let them share with the world. His design intention was to help them connect with and unleash more of their talent, even more of themselves. This showed up, sometimes in uncomfortable ways, in his management style, and it certainly showed up in the way he thought about products. This 'visionary empathy'—believing in a better future for the people who use your products—is an important consideration when we think about his impact on so many lives."

Products that are able to connect with users' aspirations are able to deliver better experiences. This is how products succeed—and business grows.

Empathy Improves Employee Performance

Here's another example of Google assuming that smarts trump soft skills. In 2013, the company launched Project Oxygen, a comprehensive analysis of all hiring, firing, and promotion data gathered since the company's incorporation in 1998. Leadership fully expected STEM proficiency to be directly linked to employee success. That was not the case. The study revealed six decidedly un-STEM traits that were linked to individual success: "being a good coach; communicating and listening well; possessing insights into others (including others' different values and points of view); having empathy toward and being supportive of one's colleagues; being a good critical thinker and problem solver; and being able to make connections across complex ideas."

Surprised but intrigued, Google hired "anthropologists and ethnographers to dive even deeper into the data… [and] enlarged its previous hiring practices to include humanities majors, artists, and even the MBAs that, initially, [cofounders] Brin and Page viewed with disdain."

Clearly, even in a company as enormous and innovation-driven as Google, empathetic employees rise to the top.

Empathetic Brands—and Workplaces— Appeal to Millennials and Gen Z

Ah, millennials. Whether your company is trying to attract more highly desirable millennial talent or tap into the huge buying power of millennial customers, one thing is certain: millennials are loyal to companies and brands that care and make a difference.

Millennial professionals are "the most traditionally diverse generation in history," according to a 2015 Deloitte leadership study. "Only 59% of millennials are Caucasian and 27% have immigrant backgrounds." And Gen Z following closely behind them raises the bar even higher in terms of what they expect in their workplaces. Organizations must understand that these younger professionals define diversity much more broadly than merely gender and race. They expect *cognitive diversity*: "a diversity of thoughts, ideas, philosophies, and in solving business problems through the culture of collaboration." And that's good news for organizations: this generation "frames diversity as a means to a business outcome" and not merely "through the lens of morality." They seek out diverse viewpoints, expertise, and talents in order to solve tough business challenges. To accommodate this type of diversity means more than just hiring people who don't look like you. It means getting to know them and listening to their point of view. Ergo, empathy.

According to a World Economic Forum article, 71 percent of millennials want their coworkers to be like a "second family," and 75 percent of them believe that their employer should mentor and nurture their innate talents. This generation craves a different kind of working experience, one in which their input is valued, their community is fostered, and their employers care about creating a better world.

"The shift we are seeing is not slight; it's momentous," Rebecca Friese Rodskog, cofounder and managing partner of FutureLeaderNow, says with no hint of exaggeration. "Good, high-performing individuals have choices, lots of employment choices that generations before did not. Among other things, the gig economy and affordable access to technology has created these opportunities. Additionally, 60 percent of millennials are open to new job opportunities—and only 29 percent of them are engaged at work. Many of them disengage when they feel they are not understood, respected, or listened to—the basic ingredients of an empathetic culture. This is a recipe for disaster for companies looking to retain their future workforce and succeed."

In this climate, engaging employees is crucial if companies want to attract and keep the best talent. Experts like Friese Rodskog see that when the organization's leaders, culture, and external brand align more closely with their employees' values, engagement is strong.

According to Erica Dhawan, the leading authority on Connectional Intelligence and founder and CEO of Cotential, we are connected in a way where voices can be heard more quickly and be more recognized, from whatever level or age. This proliferation of voices has enabled millennials to contribute their views, and, because of that, organizational leaders are required to build a more empathetic culture.

"This is no longer an *opportunity* for organizations: it's now a *required obligation* for future competitiveness, in order to retain and engage top talent," says Dhawan. "These generations were raised from childhood to university in an environment where there is so much more work being done around empathy. They are wired to think this way as a business advantage. And they won't go work for organizations that don't behave this way."

Why does it matter if workers feel invested and engaged? Because disengagement is costly. Studies by the Smith School of Business at Queen's University and Gallup showed that disengaged workers had 37 percent higher absenteeism and a whopping 60 percent more working errors. (Don't like your job? Why bother doing your best work?) Not only that, "companies with low employee engagement scores experienced 18 percent lower productivity, 16 percent lower profitability, 37 percent lower job growth, and 65 percent lower share price over time." On the flip side, "businesses with highly engaged employees received 100 percent more job applications."

As consumers, millennials have garnered a reputation for being fiscally stingy and relentlessly fickle, but a 2018 Accenture study found that this generation is actually staunchly loyal... but only to brands that make them feel valued. Millennials demand a customer-centric shopping experience, one tailored to their wants and needs as valued customers, one that proves to them that the brands they support are capable of consumer empathy.

Go beyond millennials to Gen Z (those born from 1995 onward), and empathy becomes even more important. This group values authenticity and connection in the face of a very uncertain world. According to a report put together by the Brand Team for Consumer Apps at Google, Gen Z "never knew the world before the Internet—before everything you could ever need was one click away. They never knew the world before terrorism or global warming. As a result, Gen Z is the most informed, evolved, and empathetic generation of its kind."

Empathy Drives Sales, Growth, and Market Performance

The best and most progressive corporations have begun to adopt and employ mindfully compassionate business tactics. Doing so has only improved their standing in the market.

Brighton Jones is a truly innovative wealth management company headquartered in Seattle with offices in four other cities throughout the United States. Cofounders Charles Brighton and Jon Jones wanted to break the rules and create a new role for financial planners: being the CFO for clients' lives.

With that goal in mind, the company's director of compassion (yes, they have one, as it's that important to the business)

Cory Custer has implemented an internal program called MESI, which stands for mindfulness-based emotional and social intelligence, that focuses the company culture around an empathetic and compassionate mindset. Brighton Jones hires people who are on board with this mindset, and it is currently rolling out MESI workshops for their clients and community as well. While not their driving force, they have reaped the benefits of creating an empathetic brand through their philosophy and actions. By acting with empathy through compassionate acts both for each other and their clients, Brighton Jones has achieved bottom-line success and leads the market. In fact, Brighton Jones has been recognized as a top independent advisory firm by *Barron's*, *Financial Advisor* magazine, and the *Financial Times*, among other publications. It is the largest wealth management firm in Washington State. And the firm serves nearly 2,000 individuals and families, totaling more than $8 billion assets under advisement.

"The best any of us can do is be proof statements and show the world a type of leadership, a type of business that can be compassionate and competitive," says Custer. "We're among the best registered investment advisors in the country and we intend to stay that way and not lose our heart and soul in the process. These things are not mutually exclusive—you can do well by doing good and we like to say that we're out to prove that you can be competitive and compassionate in business."

IT SHOULD BE clear by now that empathy means business. This book is meant to show you how to take deliberate action on the individual, internal culture, and external brand levels to transform your workplace into an empathetic organization. But before we dig into mindsets and tactics, let's talk a bit more about the concept of faking empathy, or what I like to call the *empathy veneer*.

Sharpen Your Empathy Edge

Empathy has been shown to have a direct impact on everything from customer loyalty to innovation to profits. Here are some of the proven benefits.

- **Empathy spurs innovation:** When you understand your customers, you can keep pace with changing needs and desires. Google's Project Aristotle found that their most innovative and profitable ideas came from teams leading with soft skills, such as empathy.
- **Empathy aligns you with customer wants and needs:** The more in tune you are with your customers, the faster you can deliver best-fit products or services before your competitors catch on. In order to know what customers desire, you must see things from their perspective. Building an ideal customer profile will help you know what their life is like. Steve Jobs, for instance, focused on understanding a customer so well that Apple's product designers knew what the customer wanted before they did.
- **Empathy improves employee performance:** Employees with more empathy and collaboration skills can often outperform and advance faster than those with purely the technical skills to succeed. Google's Project Oxygen found that having soft skills aided in team members' individual successes.
- **Empathetic brands—and workplaces—appeal to millennials and Gen Z:** As professionals, they are among the most diverse generations in the workforce and seek to leverage diverse perspectives to solve tough business challenges. They stick with employers who embrace new perspectives and value their points of view. As consumers, they're loyal to companies and brands that care and make a difference.

- **Empathy drives sales, growth, and market performance:** The best and most progressive corporations have begun to adopt and employ compassionate business tactics, which have improved their standing in the market. Brighton Jones adopted this philosophy, and it's now one of the leaders in the wealth management industry.

3

THE EMPATHY VENEER

Authentic brands don't emerge from marketing cubicles or advertising agencies. They emanate from everything the company does.
HOWARD SCHULTZ

B E WARNED: today's brand-savvy customers can spot fake empathy a mile off, and that's where they'll stay—far away from your business. Many companies have seen how empathy breeds loyalty and are eager to cash in on the benefits but reluctant to do the work. These folks slap a coat of faux-empathy over their true intentions and tactics, hoping that no one will notice its insincerity. But people notice. And the repercussions of fake empathy can be disastrous.

Belinda Parmar, who runs The Empathy Business, a consulting firm in the UK dedicated to measuring and managing empathy levels within organizations, and her team have developed a measurement tool for empathy. Each year, it publishes a list of the most empathetic companies, "an index based on an analysis of the internal culture, CEO performance, ethics, and social media presence of 170 companies on major financial indexes." In researching and interviewing representatives from these companies, Parmar has become familiar with disingenuous acts of empathy at the corporate level, which she calls "empathy-washing" and defines as a desire to appear empathetic without the right leadership, appetite for change, or sustainable, concrete actions in place to support that desire.

"When we go in on day one," says Parmar, "we're looking at what happens when we leave. Do we set up a unit, a measurements structure? What will we put in place that will allow the company to truly change so it isn't a pet project of one enlightened individual? That's always the challenge: how do you make it core to the business and how do you sustain it?"

In my own brand strategy work with growth businesses and startups, this mandate to authentically be what you say you are, and do what you say you do, takes center stage. An organization of any size or ilk—from personal brands to non-profits to global corporations—cannot simply claim a brand attribute, such as empathy (or transparency or honesty...take your pick of the brand attribute du jour), and expect people to believe it. If actions fail to back up claims, the customer's or employee's actual experience will quickly reveal the truth. When that happens, anger and disappointment soon follow.

For example, I've worked with technology companies that say they want to be seen as "innovative," which is great, if indeed they truly *are* innovative. Their desire to present their brand as "the next Apple" is admirable in theory, but if they are not willing to take the actions that Apple takes to *be Apple*, they're left with empty marketing promises. You cannot claim to be an innovative company if you have not introduced a new product in ten years, rely on outdated office technology, or refuse to invest in research or superior design. Those are the actions that back up Apple's claims of innovation.

To truly fulfill any brand promise, an organization must walk its talk, both internally and externally. Likewise, if it wants to build a brand that is seen as empathetic, but it focuses solely on good press or optics and refuses to commit to real action, its claims will soon be proven false.

Companies like United Airlines have learned hard lessons in promising empathy but failing to deliver. For years, the company has attempted to let advertising do the job of convincing flyers that exceptional customer service is its core value. But from my own experiences flying the airline and even my husband's experience as a MileagePlus Gold member, we have found that not to be the case. We have dealt with more than our fair share of surly gate agents, inflexible policies, and rude flight attendants. For example, an employee at the United lounge at London Heathrow Airport's international terminal told my husband he could bring me in with him for a ridiculously expensive guest fee but would not allow an extra guest: our two-year-old in a stroller.

The world soon learned the same thing when, in 2017, a paying customer was dragged off the plane and even injured by Chicago Department of Aviation security officers when he refused to deplane. The reason he was asked to leave? The flight was oversold and one of United's crew members needed the seat. United's flight personnel handled the situation poorly from start to finish, which then escalated with them calling airport police on their paying customer. While the flight crew did not inflict the physical harm, their decision to prioritize crew over customer and their failure to empathize with the customer's plight (he was a doctor needing to return home for appointments) offers a stark lesson in perception versus reality.

Contrast this with Southwest Airlines' friendly and approachable brand promise. The airline's brand prides itself on friendly customer service, and it actually delivers. Through everything from witty safety announcements to policies that deliver on its Transfarency® philosophy (no hidden fees, no extra baggage fees), the company exudes empathy for its patrons. Southwest continues to give out free in-flight snacks, even though most airlines no longer do this. And the crew has been trained to think on their feet, a sign that the company strives to hire the right, quick-thinking, empathetic people. We'll talk about such hiring practices later in the book.

I flew Southwest with my son on the day of his third birthday. The flight attendant found out mid-flight, and, without telling me, the crew whipped up a "birthday cake" for him, made of plastic cups, napkin banners, extra snack treats, and toothpicks holding the whole masterpiece together. They saw things from a kid's point of view—spending his birthday trapped on a plane—and took action. My son was delighted and I, of course, was deeply appreciative. Little gestures like these can have a huge impact.

No matter where your organization is right now, the eventual goal is to create a brand and culture rooted in genuine empathy, the true test of which comes during hard times. It's one thing to be understanding and see things from another's perspective when the company is doing well, you get along with all your coworkers, and your customers are blissfully happy at every waking moment. But a company with an empathy veneer won't pass the test in the face of employee conflict, system collapse, or the loss of a huge client.

Dave Ballai is chief information officer (CIO) and vice-president of content operations for Reed Tech, a LexisNexis company that provides information-based solutions and services to clients all over the world, particularly government agencies, the intellectual property market, and the life sciences industry. He leads a team of 150 people, not counting his contractors and vendors. Ballai believes that maintaining an empathetic stance during emergencies is all about determining if your organization and its leaders are truly empathetic or merely paying it lip service. "When things are difficult," he says, "you really test the true mettle of a leader and you know whether or not that leader is honestly empathetic or is only practicing because there's no pressure to do otherwise," he says.

While backing up empathetic claims with action grows dividends, slapping a false veneer of empathy on your brand will backfire spectacularly. So, what can you do to avoid this mistake?

The following questions will help you ensure your organization is acting empathetically at every level—leadership, culture, and external brand. This means everything from hiring the right people to managing meetings more effectively to rewarding the right behaviors to understanding customers and adapting to their needs. Focus on these things first, and then move on to doing good in the community and making your empathy visible outside company walls.

To ensure you're infusing empathy in a holistic way, ask yourself:

1   **Are we aligned on mission and values?** Does everyone inside and outside of the organization understand our story, values, and purpose? And is this translating to what we're presenting externally, in our marketing messages and customer service? If you can't internally articulate this, you can't operationalize any of it or make it effective. (More on this in chapters 7 and 9.)

2   **What internal policies or practices are in place to foster empathy?** Do we reward empathy and collaboration? Do we make this part of our performance reviews? What are

our policies for running meetings, getting to know each other as colleagues, welcoming new hires, preparing new managers, managing conflict, and mentoring emerging leaders? (More on this in chapter 7.)

3 **Are we building a safe and trusting environment?** Can our people openly collaborate without feeling like they have to be competitive? Do they also have the flexibility to take calculated risks or make tough decisions on the fly without fear of failure? (More on this in chapters 5 and 7.)

4 **Are we "hiring right"?** Do we have the right leaders in place who have the emotional intelligence as well as the business acumen to deliver long-term results? How about the right people in customer service, representing the brand? Do we screen for high emotional intelligence (emotional quotient, or EQ)? (More on this in chapters 5, 7, and 9.)

5 **Do we implement proactive and flexible customer service policies?** These policies should be based on trust and offer the benefit of the doubt. Do we assume the best in customers with policies that support them? Do we give customer-facing employees the opportunity to think on their feet and personalize solutions based on customer needs in the moment? (More on this in chapter 9.)

You can download a free Empathy Authenticity Checklist and review it with your leadership team from www.theempathyedge.com/resources.

Now that we've described what empathy is, and what it isn't, let's explore the benefits of an empathetic leader and then how you can flex that muscle in the work environment—or build it if it's gone unused for a while.

Sharpen Your Empathy Edge

- Today's brand-savvy customers can spot fake empathy a mile off, and that's where they'll stay—far away from your business. The repercussions of fake empathy can be disastrous.

- To truly fulfill any brand promise, including being empathetic, an organization must walk its talk, both internally and externally. If a company wants to build a brand that is seen as empathetic, but it focuses solely on good press or optics and refuses to commit to real action, its claims will soon be proven false.

- It's one thing to be understanding and see things from another's perspective when the company is doing well. But a company with an empathy veneer won't pass the test in the face of employee conflict, system collapse, or the loss of a huge client.

To ensure your organization is infusing empathy in a holistic way, ask yourself:

1 Are we aligned on mission and values?
2 What internal policies or practices are in place to foster empathy?
3 Are we building a safe and trusting environment?
4 Are we "hiring right"?
5 Do we implement proactive and flexible customer service policies?

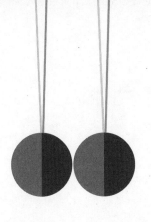

PART II

THE
EMPATHETIC
LEADER

4

BENEFITS OF EMPATHETIC LEADERS

Measure your impact in humanity not in the likes
but the lives you touch; not in popularity but in the people
you serve... There will be times when your resolve to serve
humanity will be tested. Be prepared. People will try to
convince you that you should keep your empathy out of
your career. Don't accept this false premise.

TIM COOK, CEO OF APPLE

A Catalyst for Entrepreneurship

Joy McBrien longed to make a difference in the world. In college, she tested several ideas for a social entrepreneurship venture that would improve the lives of women who were victims of sexual violence. This was not just an idealistic whim: McBrien had survived sexual assault and strongly empathized with other women who could not escape such circumstances. Her own assaults had shaped her identity, and she had spent much of her time in college trying to process her experiences.

"I started traveling and meeting with women because of my own history of sexual violence and I was struggling to be able to talk to people about it in the U.S. because of the stigma associated with it," she explains.

This search for empathy around assault led her to Peru, where, at the age of nineteen, she helped local women build a shelter for domestic violence victims. McBrien expected this experience to be transformative, but she got a big slap in the face. She realized that her motivations weren't entirely selfless, and she might even be offering these women the wrong kind of help. "The shelter was important and sorely needed, but I realized that if I was going to do anything of real value in these communities, I need to understand the people there much more, the context of their daily lives," she says.

According to the World Health Organization, between 51 percent and 69 percent of women living in Peru's major cities have been raped or assaulted by a partner. McBrien was driven to help them but wanted to be strategic. She returned home to the U.S. and began formulating a plan.

McBrien returned to Peru over the next few summers, as coordinated through a non-profit called Friends of Chimbote, with a singular focus to learn as much as she could. She met with rural village women who had experienced sexual violence to learn what they were doing in their own communities to address this huge problem. They told her that jobs were the single most important resource for women experiencing domestic violence, because sustainable income helped empower them to leave their abusive partners.

McBrien decided she could address two problems at once.

With the help of a local Peruvian social worker known affectionately as Anita, McBrien started an artisan group in Chimbote that cleverly doubled as a domestic violence support group. Most sexual abuse in Peru happens inside the home, and the women coping with this persistent violence were not talking about it or sharing resources. McBrien's idea was to empower the women with marketable skills while simultaneously giving them a safe place to talk about their experiences. The artisan group got together to crochet for four hours each week, with all materials provided to them for free courtesy of McBrien's creative fundraising. At the end of each session, they had a hat to keep or sell at the market and a better understanding of how their neighbors were dealing with abusive spouses and partners. They built relationships, skills, and confidence.

Seeing the potential for a business model, McBrien recognized that the best way for these women to make real money on their crafts was to sell them in the U.S. So, based on her experience running a jewelry business, she switched the artisanal focus to jewelry to make the products more marketable and created the company Fair Anita to link the Peruvian crafters to American buyers. Fair Anita served as facilitator and middleman, providing everything from design input to shipping infrastructure. It was a roaring success.

Today, Fair Anita is a booming social enterprise that sells trendy, affordable, fair trade products made by more than 8,000 talented yet marginalized women in nine countries spread across Africa, Asia, and South America. McBrien's company partners with female artisan collectives and provides them with fair wages, long-term employment, and business development opportunities. Not all artisan groups follow the domestic violence–support model, but all generate income for women that helps them respond to violent gender dynamics in their community. Fair Anita was incorporated as a Minnesota Public Benefit Corporation on January 2, 2015, and by the end of 2017, McBrien had exceeded her sales goals by 200 percent and posted sales of nearly $500,000 for the year.

She started with her own experiences, used them to spark empathy, and designed a business model that served her desire to help while turning a profit and empowering at-risk women across the globe. Joy McBrien is the quintessential empathetic leader.

And Fair Anita is a perfect example of how empathy can spark entrepreneurship. Some businesses are founded by a single person who's had a transformative experience, and that person's drive to help the world is what fuels the business. Others are created by a visionary who sees pain or suffering in the world and reacts to it by creating a company that facilitates action. Either way, it's clear that pairing empathy with entrepreneurship can yield spectacular results.

That said, not all empathetic leaders are founders, entrepreneurs, or even executives. Leading with empathy can happen at all levels and manifest in infinite ways. As we discussed in chapter 2, empathetic leaders cultivate lasting loyalty among their people and that loyalty leads to tangible market results. But what does empathy-driven leadership look like in practice? How do leaders of for-profit companies transform their individual empathy into company-wide compassion?

Empathy has fueled many an entrepreneur's desire to create something different, better, or more useful. One person's strong empathy for a group of people can drive the creation and expansion of an entire organization. A visionary leader who is able to put themselves in someone else's shoes can build a business with empathy at its core, lead and inspire a diverse workforce, and make real change in the world—all while earning a profit. In fact, some of the most exciting and innovative businesses in the world were founded by or are being led by those who embody empathy, resulting in an almost magical connection with their teams and customers.

Let's dig into the benefits of empathetic leadership.

More Loyalty

When leaders display genuine empathy—keeping their "interpersonal" door open, rather than talking a good game about an open-door policy—it can put their teams at ease. When the leader sets a tone of "Hey, we all see things from each other's perspective and look out for each other," it can go a long way to defusing tense office politics. Employees are more willing to accept feedback or unpopular decisions when they understand that their boss has their best interests at heart and can see their point of view. It's easier to take risks, be creative, and work harder in such a trusting environment. An employee who feels safe and understood can bring their best self to work and focus on quality over drama.

Dave Ballai of Reed Tech knows from personal experience that being supportive and compassionate toward his team members pays off. In fact, his leadership philosophy is rooted in empathy. "In any role, your success is going to be directly correlated to the success of your team—not just the people who are paying for your services but also the ones who are working hard to provide them," he explains. "Those people, your team members, need the highest level of understanding and support... I have no hesitation about seeing someone in an organization grow to a role above the role that I'm in, in any organization hierarchy. I think that's the best compliment that an organization can pay to its leaders—it's not about the compensation; it's about sharing and helping others. In the long run, it's the real return."

The empathy-loyalty link is undeniable when leaders model and express genuine empathy. Plus, leaders who take the time to get to know their employees and customers, see things from their perspectives, and *act accordingly* are far better poised to achieve their own goals.

Decisiveness

You might think that those who lead with empathy are more indecisive because they try to please everyone. That is not the case. Empathy does not mean "caving" to the demands of all stakeholders, but empathetic leaders do try to find a good balance by considering all viewpoints and then making informed decisions. They collect information, consider, and act decisively.

Renee Metty is the founder of With Pause, a company that coaches entrepreneurs, executives, teams, and school leaders on how to adopt mindfulness practices to perform better and live life with more purpose. She has worked with companies such as AT&T, Microsoft, and Citrix. Empathy plays a big role in her work, and she insists that the empathetic leaders and individuals she works with are *more*, not less, decisive than others.

"Those who have empathy can look at that team member who is not performing or that teammate who's driving everyone crazy and have some understanding about what their home situation is or how much they have on their plate," she says. "They are able to shift their perspective about them and then take thoughtful action."

With empathy, a leader can be more compassionate toward and connected to that person in order to accomplish the organization's goals.

"When you can see people as human beings versus pawns on a chess board, then you can act compassionately," says Metty. "And sometimes that may mean letting the person go. You might be able to see that the reason this person is failing to deliver is that they are not in the right role or that the work they are doing is making them miserable."

In this way, empathetic leaders are able to see the big picture from multiple angles and make critical decisions from an informed perspective.

Agility and Connection

For a business to be successful, groups of people from diverse viewpoints must come together to solve problems and achieve goals. Those interpersonal relationships are key, and no amount of process redesign or slick technology can make a dysfunctional team perform at maximum power. For a leader to enable healthy, efficient teams, they must be aware of employee needs and interpersonal politics. Leaders must listen, hear, and process what's happening among the ranks.

Jayson Boyers, president and CEO of Cleary University, learned early in his career that empathy is the key to engaging employees and helping them forge productive team dynamics. This insight enabled him to unearth ideas and lead people effectively through change. In a powerful *Forbes* article, he writes:

> Early in my career, I learned the power of empathy to break down barriers and open doors. I was responsible for overseeing my company's largest division, which needed drastic improvements from a state of poor employee morale, lack of trust in leadership, and customer retention issues. Rather than force my will and clean house, I sat down with each employee to gauge their feelings about the company and talk about how to improve results. Through empathetic employee engagement, we could create a pathway to success.
>
> I wish I could say that there was a complete turnaround, but some employees felt that they would be happier elsewhere. We never stopped talking about what needed to be done, though—those who stayed knew that I was always open to new ideas. Giving others an outlet to express their thoughts, even when we disagreed, gave people a vested interest in the company's direction and success.

The lesson here? Empathetic leaders are constantly attuned to the needs of their teams as well as the customers they serve, which equips them to react better and faster to make those relationships more productive. They can meet people where they are and consider various viewpoints when making decisions. When you understand how an individual learns, how they process feedback, or even what motivates them, you can adapt your leadership tactics to empower them to perform at their best. With a willingness to see and hear other perspectives, empathetic leaders can make better decisions.

This agility and willingness to see other points of view before making decisions doesn't just improve internal relationships, it also leads to happier external customers. We all know that making decisions in an ivory tower, with no customer insight or input, can lead to the creation of products no one wants to buy. Experts get caught in a "I know what's best" trap and fail to innovate as workplaces evolve, markets shift, or customers change.

Adaptability

Being an empathetic leader can make you more open to changing customer needs and enable you to adapt with more confidence. When you create a healthy dialogue—whether with your own internal team or your external stakeholders—new ideas can take root. You get continuous feedback and input. You are able to ensure that your products change and grow to meet new customer needs.

"Business success depends on empathetic leaders who are able to adapt, build on the strengths around them, and relate to their environment," Boyers insists. "When businesses fail, it is often because leaders have stopped focusing on understanding their environment intimately and instead stay insulated in their own operations. Successful business leaders are receptive to disruption and innately aware of what is going on in their organizations both internally and externally."

Remember Jon Jones, CEO and cofounder of Brighton Jones, the wealth management firm based in Seattle? He structured his company to consider wealth management more holistically than the rest of the industry, seeing the company's role as helping clients live a richer life: financially, mentally, and physically. Seeing the world through their client's eyes enabled the founders to adapt their business model and build a company with a unique approach to client service.

The old model of an advisor who only offers products for which they are compensated never sat right with them, even though it was accepted as standard industry practice. There was a gap in the marketplace, an opportunity for empathetic wealth managers to become true personal CFOs for their clients rather than commissioned sales reps. In talking with clients, Jones and his cofounder Charles Brighton discovered that many had doubts about whether a financial advisor was really looking out for their interests or simply lining their own pockets.

"I saw that people in the financial industry focused on product; there's advice but there's advice with 'and by the way, this is what you should buy,'" says Jones. "I felt like there are great products out there and crappy products out there, and our clients are busy enough that they didn't want to have to spend the time to wade through all the information. They want to be able to trust that our recommendations are in their best interests and just move forward."

By leveraging this insight, Jones led his company toward a desirable and profitable niche. Brighton Jones listened to client concerns, created a business model that could shift and adapt to their needs, and built a reputation on being empathetic. And it's served them well, as you saw in their impressive sales and growth numbers in chapter 2. After getting its start less than two decades ago as a two-person shop, Brighton Jones now has more than 175 employees with additional offices in Portland, San Francisco, Scottsdale, and Washington, D.C. Not to mention, Brighton Jones is a "Best Companies to Work For" honoree eleven years running—a streak no other Washington State organization has matched.

THE BENEFITS OF empathetic leadership are many and powerful. Now that you know what they are, you're likely keen to learn how to cultivate and amplify them in yourself or the leaders around you. Read on to explore ways to tailor leadership to reflect empathy and create compassion.

Sharpen Your Empathy Edge

Leaders at every level can propel an organization and brand to become more empathetic. But being an empathetic leader also offers numerous benefits for the individual.

- **Empathy can be a catalyst for entrepreneurship:** Some businesses are founded by a single person who's had a transformative experience; that person's drive to help the world fuels the business. Other businesses are created by a visionary who sees pain or suffering and reacts to it by creating a company that facilitates action. Joy McBrien created Fair Anita as a way to give women a safe space to talk about their experiences while supporting them in selling their crafts in the marketplace.
- **Empathetic leaders engender loyalty:** Leaders who display genuine empathy can put their teams at ease. Leaders who

take the time to get to know their employees and customers, see things from their perspectives, and act accordingly are far better poised to achieve their own goals.

- **Empathetic leaders can make good decisions:** They collect information from various perspectives, consider their options, and act decisively. They are able to see the big picture from multiple angles and make critical decisions from an informed perspective.
- **Empathetic leaders are agile and connected:** They are constantly attuned to the needs of their teams as well as the customers they serve, which equips them to react better and faster to make those relationships more productive. They can meet people where they are, motivate them based on individual preferences, and consider various viewpoints when making decisions.
- **Empathetic leaders are adaptable:** Being an empathetic leader can make you more open to changing customer needs and enable you to adapt with more confidence. When you create a healthy dialogue—whether with your own internal team or your external stakeholders—new ideas can take root. You get continuous feedback and input. You are able to adjust your actions and ensure that your products change and grow to meet new customer needs.

5

HABITS AND TRAITS OF EMPATHETIC LEADERS

How to Flex Your Empathy Muscles to Lead More Effectively

*Leadership is about empathy. It is about having
the ability to relate to and connect with people for the
purpose of inspiring and empowering their lives.*

OPRAH WINFREY

LEADERSHIP CAN TAKE many forms within an organization, and empathy can be expressed in many ways. So, how do you personally work to lead empathetically? What can you do at your level to cultivate empathy within your company's existing culture? And what if you just don't feel like a naturally empathetic person?

First, don't panic. Research has shown that empathy is innate to humans and vital to our survival; how much of it you exhibit depends on how often you've had the opportunity to flex and develop that muscle throughout your life. If you are keen to reap the benefits of empathetic leadership, just remember that even seemingly skeptical Paul Bloom, author of *Against Empathy*, believes that "empathy is more than a reflex. It can be nurtured, stanched, developed, and extended through the imagination."

With that in mind, here are seven simple ways to train yourself to lead more empathetically.

1. Practice Presence

If you feel constantly scattered and preoccupied, you'll have no capacity to consider others' perspectives or think clearly. You'll be in defensive and reactive mode constantly, which is the antithesis of empathy—you'll be too caught up in your own "stuff" to listen to anyone else!

Dr. Zanette Johnson, whom we first met in chapter 1, works with organizations to design routines, rituals, and practices that help them reach and sustain their goals. She teaches the neuroscience of mindful and effective leadership and, in her workshops, uses hands-on exercises for addressing the perils of reactivity.

"One of the things that comes up consistently with my clients is that there's so much power in gaining control over our reactive impulses—doing that allows us to make better choices, to respond in alignment with our intention," Johnson says. "That plays a pivotal role in acting with empathy and compassion."

Mindfulness coach Renee Metty agrees. "There's a lot of awareness that can happen when you start looking at your own emotions and thoughts in a given situation and determining what your triggers are," says Metty. Your own experiences and conditioning can cause you to project onto others, rather than see what is going on for *them* or driving their behavior. And that can be a huge impediment to acting with empathy.

Metty finds that leaders and individuals who develop a mindfulness practice, however small, are more grounded, more in tune with their colleagues and teams, and better able to be empathetic and act with compassion.

Being present and mindful does not have to slow you down. Many of Metty's clients are high performers. She herself is a type A overachiever who's on the go all the time, but it wasn't until she slowed down that she found her sweet spot and her edge as an entrepreneur and high performer herself. (Talk about empathy for her own clients!) In addition to serving clients, speaking nationally, and running her business, Metty also founded and runs a successful preschool in Seattle that practices mindfulness education.

"Mindfulness is not a silver bullet," Metty warns. "But it is a gateway. As you become fully aware, if you don't do anything with that awareness, then what's the point? You can notice a bunch of stuff, but if you're still operating on old default patterns, why bother?"

If you want to act with more empathy, compassion, and understanding at work, then jump-start that action by taking a step back, being present, and slowing down.

"There's a part of the brain that corrects for the overactive ego and narcissistic self-thinking. One of the things that activates that part of our brains is being calm," says Johnson. "If we're in a state of emotional arousal for any reason, that 'corrective' part of the brain doesn't do its thing. We literally can't empathize deeply with others when we're under the influence of our emotions."

How do you begin to practice presence so you can make room for empathy? The key is to start small. "It's called a 'practice' for a reason," Metty says.

Many leaders cite discipline and commitment as key to their success, but mindfulness can be equally powerful, especially if it becomes part of an ingrained success routine, like a daily morning workout or reading habit. The key is to be consistent and pick something you can stick with. "I emphasize daily practice versus a set length of time," Metty says. "It takes away the negotiation of skipping a day and 'doing it tomorrow.'"

Even five minutes is a good start. If you can commit to five minutes daily instead of thirty minutes weekly, commit to the five minutes. Once you're consistent, practice begets practice. And when you start to see the results in how you handle conflict, see another's perspective, and act with compassion, the results will speak for themselves.

Here are some mindfulness practices you can try for five or ten minutes a day to see what works best for your personal style.

- Sit in silence and notice where your mind goes.
- Meditate (whatever that means to you).
- Breathe deeply and slowly, focusing on your exhalations and inhalations.
- Knit.
- Journal.
- Walk, stretch, or take a quick jog.

Schedule the time in your calendar and hold it sacred.

In terms of cultivating mindfulness in the presence of others, start by avoiding distractions. Put away your phone, don't glance at email. Do this in all your meetings, and encourage everyone else to do the same. Don't multitask. Turn off your monitor during one-on-ones. Create an environment that allows singular concentration and respectful focus.

Lisa Reynolds is the vice-president of talent management for CHRISTUS Health, a healthcare organization based in Irving, Texas, with facilities across Texas, Louisiana, New

Mexico, as well as Mexico, Chile, and Colombia. It has more than 42,000 employees in the U.S. and Latin America and runs sixty hospitals and more than 300 physician clinics, stand-alone clinics, and emergency rooms.

One of CHRISTUS Health's core values is compassion, which they define as service in the spirit of empathy, love, and concern. They hire people specifically with such traits and tendencies. Reynolds has vast experience in hiring and training leaders to be successful.

"What I've observed in working with leaders that are empathetic is that they're present," says Reynolds, "so when somebody has a need, they're not scrolling through their cell phone reading emails or typing on their computer. They're fully present."

2. Listen More, Stay Humble

Presence can be somewhat passive, but empathy requires you to actively listen and hear what is going on for someone else. You cannot do this if you are talking all the time. Instead of always charging in with "This is what I think you should do," ask for input and reflect on the response you receive.

Empathetic leadership requires restraint to listen to people's experiences, stories, and perspectives and draw patterns from that information, over and over again.

Believe me, I'm no prize when it comes to consistently doing this. I'm one of those people who so badly wants to help the team solve a problem that I sometimes forget they have valid (and often better) ideas, too. But it's amazing how much easier it gets when you consciously enter conversations with an active listening mindset. (I call this my internal "shusher": *Hush up and listen!*)

Dave Ballai, chief information officer and vice-president of content operations for Reed Tech, is particularly troubled by how entrepreneurial leaders in particular fail to listen. "There are not a lot of empathetic entrepreneurs out there," he says. "Either they're so academic that they can't see past the end of the textbook or they're so politically driven that they don't have the sensitivity for others. There are precious few who have the ability to listen to and resonate with others' thoughts. It takes a lot of patience in an environment where there's a lot of pressure."

It also takes a mindset shift away from goals-driven leadership toward impact-centric leadership. Being a leader who listens means valuing the solution that creates the most positive change, regardless of its source. Being a leader who listens means seeing yourself as a servant, not a dictator.

One way that Reed Tech fosters this connection between listening and humility is through volunteering. "Our management team is encouraged to join boards," Ballai says. "I've been on non-profit boards and chaired them; it really does help to promote that servant-leader orientation."

Cory Custer, director of compassion for Brighton Jones, encourages both active listening and humility in leaders. "There's a way to lead or consult in which you say, 'I am the expert; let me show you the way,'" he says. "There's another way to lead, which is far more compelling, and that's to say, 'Hey, I'm no kind of expert in this area; I'm learning. I think there's a lot to be said for focusing on emotional and social intelligence and I'd like to invite you all to join me.' And that's more authentic."

When leaders talk constantly and bulldoze other speakers, they broadcast callousness. When leaders talk less and listen more, the message they send is that opinions other than their own actually matter. These humble servant-leaders are relatable, approachable, and inspirational.

Practice active listening. Let people vent, talk, and express themselves before you jump in with your responses. Don't champ at the bit waiting for your turn to speak; pay attention to the information you're being given. Doing so will give you access to a wealth of insight that your colleagues and direct reports are eager to share.

3. Be Curious

According to Roman Krznaric, author of *Empathy: Why It Matters, and How to Get It,* one of the key traits of highly empathic people (HEPs) is that they have an insatiable curiosity about strangers. They find other people more interesting than themselves, and HEPs are eager to learn about lives and worldviews different from their own. Their natural openness helps them understand the world from multiple perspectives.

Fair Anita founder Joy McBrien's curiosity is what led to her breakthrough social enterprise idea. To improve the lives of domestic violence victims in poor rural areas of the world and find a business idea that would best serve them, McBrien spent six years traveling and meeting with women from approximately sixteen countries, because she wanted to learn more about what violence against women looks like in different cultural contexts. She honed her social enterprise ideas while keeping an open mind. "It was all about 'Don't go with your ideas.' Spend the first half learning and listening and then see where you can add value," she says.

Without this respectful curiosity, she never would have learned, for example, that the artisans needed to work from home to protect their children or that they took pride in building connections with their end customers halfway across the world. If she hadn't focused on being open to their input and perspectives, she wouldn't have discovered that they were so eager to expand her project that they'd help take the reins and create opportunities for other women in their villages.

While focused in the corporate realm, Kim Bohr agrees with this approach. As founder and CEO of The Innovare Group, a boutique strategic consultancy that helps organizations boost profits, performance, and team passion, she steers her clients away from presumption and toward inquisitiveness. Her work with for-profit executives is strongly informed by bringing empathy, curiosity, and leadership development into client strategy. Only by including those in the operational solution can executives develop the right leadership behavior so problems don't occur again.

"When working to solve a complex operational problem, we always talk about confronting an issue without laying judgment and blame. The whole purpose of that is to have a mindset of curiosity and real desire to help someone grow. To open the conversation, say, 'I've been seeing this "recurring behavior" and I'm concerned,'" she says. "To say, 'I want to talk about the issue so that I can understand. This conversation isn't about blame. It's important for me to get really curious and learn from you, so I can become more empathetic to what's going on and we can find a solution together. What help or support do you or the team need to achieve what we're trying to do or change that behavior?'"

She also warns that advice can become the antithesis of curiosity. "If we're always in advice-giving mode and not asking questions, we're training people to avoid thinking for themselves," Bohr explains. "Yes, it might feel like a faster resolution but we're doing them a disservice... It's natural to think, *If this worked for me, it should work for you*, [but it] is not likely the right result. It works better to hold this place of genuine curiosity that allows somebody to be guided through their own self-discovery and really help them dig deeper.

Being empathetic gives them space to own their decisions and outcomes."

Are there times you need to be decisive and swift? Absolutely. Nothing drives a team battier than an indecisive leader who constantly requires consensus before acting. But if you prudently choose empathy as your input gathering mode before making a final decision, the team will notice—even if the decision is not the one that certain individuals wanted you to make. And all that listening will pay off later because you will better understand how to communicate that decision and deliver the message for the best team result.

4. Explore with Your Imagination

If you want to be more empathetic, you have to practice walking in other people's shoes. But since it's not possible (or advisable) to follow your employees home every night, or visit with every one of your thousands of global customers, you have to be a little creative. Consuming stories that offer diverse viewpoints is a great way to get inside the minds of others and play with what that feels like for you.

Read historical nonfiction, biographies, and fiction written by authors who come from different racial, gender, or economic backgrounds. Watch documentaries about people in far-off lands or in dramatically different socio-economic circumstances than you. Travel to a place where the residents don't speak your language (and not simply via a cruise ship's three-hour port of call). Immerse yourself in music, food, and art from another country.

As an actress in my spare time, I believe there is no better playground for empathy than film and theater, when you are literally immersed in the experiences and emotions of others in the moment. Characters are often in situations you've never experienced or come from backgrounds you might barely understand. Live theater in particular offers an opportunity to pull up a seat outside someone's window and peek into their world in real time. It can transform you. If you're as much a fan of live theater as my husband (who will only attend if I'm in the play and even then begrudgingly), opt for narrative films or documentaries. Be brave and branch out to something beyond flighty rom-coms or slapstick comedies every now and then.

Here's an example of how imaginative exploration can foster empathetic urges—and lead to successful entrepreneurial leadership.

Many years ago, little Dina Buchbinder sat in her classroom in Mexico City. And she was bored. She was not the best of students and didn't understand why she had to go to school nor was she excited by what she was learning. Like any active little girl, Buchbinder preferred connecting and interacting with others, instead of passively taking notes while a teacher droned on at the chalkboard.

Then Buchbinder's middle school geography teacher, Mrs. Zaida, opened up her world. This creative teacher took the kids on "trips" inside their imaginations. They consulted the globe, picked new destinations, and learned all about the cultures and customs of that place. They wrote postcards from their imaginary travels. They learned about amazing countries, environments, and people all over the world without ever leaving their classroom. Something sparked inside of Buchbinder. Finally, it all made sense: *This is why we go to school*. We go to understand the world beyond ourselves, to see that what makes our planet great is its diversity of thought, culture, and experience. We go to puzzle out relationships between countries, between concepts, and between individuals. School done right wasn't about memorization: it was about studying context and making connections through a powerful, meaningful tool such as play.

Later, Buchbinder studied international relations at Instituto Tecnológico Autónomo de México (ITAM) and was selected to take part in a Ship for World Youth travel and exchange program, sponsored by the Japanese government. For two months, Buchbinder traveled all over the Pacific and learned about different countries and cultures. While on that trip, she befriended a woman who told her about a unique program in Canada that taught children through play.

Buchbinder was inspired. She had never forgotten that middle school teacher's creativity, and she realized that a connection to play had been what ignited her own dormant thirst for learning. She knew kids wanted to learn, but what if they were like her and felt bored by the way they were being taught? *What if*, she thought, *we could make a whole new set of tools available to future leaders and changemakers?*

When she got back to Mexico, her colleagues laughed at her idea. No one took her seriously as they pursued careers in the private and government sectors. "I had never heard the term 'social entrepreneur' in my life," Buchbinder says, with a laugh. "All I knew is that I wanted to do something different. In my heart, I needed to do something meaningful to impact the next generation. So, I just went ahead and tried it."

With a partner, Buchbinder launched Deportes para Compartir, or Sports for Sharing, in Mexico in 2007 to teach elementary school children empathy, teamwork, and cross-cultural understanding through sports and games. With barely any budget or resources, she and her partner modeled the curriculum after the Canadian program but adapted the games, stories, and strategies to better serve indigenous, rural communities. They launched a pilot in four extremely diverse areas: one indigenous community in Chihuahua, two very different private schools in Mexico City, and a public school near residential Cancún. They wanted to prove this idea would really work. And it did.

Today, Deportes para Compartir is part of a broader organization called Educación para Compartir, as they have also added art, science, digital citizenship, and an initiative that teaches children how to launch projects and create change themselves.

Buchbinder was invited to explore empathy through her imagination at a very early age, and she has gone on to found and lead an organization that encourages youngsters of all ages to embrace empathy and become changemakers. It's an elegant chain reaction: her teacher taught her to view the world with empathy, and that teaching method helped her grow into an empathetic leader who is driven to ensure it is taught to future generations.

"When you connect to people, your community, and the environment, you can understand more. You care and can solve problems, you can see multiple perspectives and solutions," says Buchbinder. "This is what we're trying to do here. Use creative approaches to turn children into empathetic, open-minded citizens who care and can find creative solutions that make the world a better place."

What can you do to explore with your imagination? Seek to discover, learn about, and understand the story of someone who is not like you. Question your assumptions as you watch or listen. Imagine what you would do in similar circumstances. Learn the stories behind a magnificent painting or haunting musical piece, then consider the artist or musician who created it and contemplate what they were feeling, what their circumstances were, or what the geo-political backdrop was at the time they created this work.

By using your imagination, you can flex those empathy muscles, so that when the everyday real races are run with coworkers, team members, or customers, you can draw on this strength. Just like muscle memory, it will get easier over time to default to that empathetic mode of thinking and interacting.

5. Cultivate Confidence

A big piece of becoming a more empathetic leader is to work on yourself first. How is your self-confidence? What is going on for you right now? Are you being empathetic and compassionate with yourself?

Sounds a little woo-woo, but it's really just common sense, similar to airline attendants instructing us to put on our own oxygen masks before helping others. To have empathy and, in turn, show compassion for others, you have to first do the same for yourself. Otherwise, as with the oxygen mask, you won't have enough air left to be of any help to anyone.

In her book *When Things Fall Apart: Heart Advice for Difficult Times*, Tibetan Buddhist nun and teacher Pema Chödrön writes, "Having compassion starts and ends with having compassion for all those unwanted parts of ourselves, all those imperfections that we don't even want to look at."

Without a healthy store of self-confidence, it becomes much harder to be present, listen, and practice curiosity because we're consumed with worry. When we're so busy doubting ourselves and fretting over negative judgments, there's no energy left to empathize with other people. According to Chödrön, "The only reason we don't open our hearts and minds to other people is that they trigger confusion in us that we don't feel brave enough or sane enough to deal with."

In other words, we avoid empathy when we lack self-confidence and succumb to fear. On the flip side, when we operate from a place of solid confidence (not arrogance, mind you), we're more able to hear and accept ideas that are contrary to our own. We're not threatened by different perspectives or out-of-the-box thinking because we trust ourselves and have faith in our abilities. Without that grounding, empathy feels dangerous. With it, empathy flows naturally.

Beyond Buddhism, companies see results in the business world when their empathetic leaders are able to put ego aside and listen to other ideas and points of view. Stacey Engle, president of Fierce Conversations, says, "As a leader, when you are making decisions, it is not about consensus. You are tasked with making the best possible decision for the organization. You need to get it right for the organization as opposed to *being* right... This means being willing to be challenged and seeking to understand other perspectives. You don't always have to agree, but you must be open."

So, how do you bolster your confidence as a leader? Well, there's no simple, one-size-fits-all answer! However, most experts agree that doing hard, challenging things and proving to yourself that you're capable of handling adversity works pretty darned well.

You can also bolster your confidence by engaging in these acts, big and small.

- **Set goals and track your progress.** Sometimes we can't always objectively see how far we've come or what we've achieved until it's in front of us in black and white (or in color, if you're into charts and graphs).

- **Celebrate your successes.** Not just at the end of a big goal but at each milestone along the way. This is imperative for momentum.

- **Conduct 360-degree assessments with your team.** This might seem counterintuitive: *Won't they just point out all my shortcomings?* Perhaps, yes. But such exercises will also highlight your strengths. Outsiders can often pinpoint our skills and talents easier than we can.

- **Keep a "high-five" file.** Tuck away all those meaningful notes of praise, gratitude, and big wins so you can revisit them when your confidence is flagging. I have a folder in my email called "Sweet Stuff" and one in my file drawer called "Inspiration." (And yes, my paper file actually includes my college scholarship and acceptance letter... sometimes you have to dig *way* back, but do whatever works!)

- **Establish an accountability partner or board of directors for yourself.** Find others who are where you want to be, or those who will hold you accountable and give you unbiased perspective. This is a great way to get honest feedback when your own self-doubt creeps in, as well as keep you improving, innovating, and growing as a leader.

- **Flip your mindset with a single mantra.** Before a big meeting, take two minutes and say to yourself, "I'm here to make a difference." Breathe. Ground yourself and then walk in. Lisa Earle McLeod is a sales leadership consultant and the author of *Selling with Noble Purpose* and *The Triangle of Truth: The Surprisingly Simple Secret to Solving Conflicts Large and Small.* She coaches her clients on this aspect and it's a game changer. "If you think, *I'm here to make a difference*, that's a different lens than *I've got to get these five things done.* You'll flip out of yourself to the other person's point of view, and you'll show up more grounded and confident."

- **Rock out.** Play songs from high points in your life, like what you jammed to in high school or when you first drove by yourself. While this might seem silly, McLeod consistently finds this helps her clients stand taller and muster more energy, because it brings them back to a time of extreme confidence. No harm in trying this if it works for you, so dig out those old Bon Jovi tunes before your next team meeting!

6. Get in the Trenches

Experiencing another's perspective by living their life for a day is sometimes called *experiential journalism*. In the television show *Undercover Boss*, a CEO throws on a disguise and goes into the trenches alongside front-line workers. It's an eye-opening experience for these leaders to see what their employees face every day when they think no one is watching and the heroic lengths they go to in order to please customers or sacrifice for their jobs. Leaders need to be in the trenches just as much as, if not more so than, their teams.

Andrew Marks is cofounder of SuccessHACKER, a management consultancy focused on helping companies improve customer satisfaction, increase customer success, and create lifetime value. They work with innovative tech companies full of smart people but also where empathy and emotional intelligence is sometimes in short supply, and they must help shift the cultural mindset.

"The best customer-success organizations have people that are empathetic, that have high EQ," says Marks. "The capacity to put yourself in somebody else's position is incredibly important to not only be able to express to that customer that you truly understand their frustrations and how they're feeling but also to express internally to your organization what you're seeing, hearing, and feeling from the customers out in the field."

Marks shared a powerful example of what happens when leaders disconnect from the customer. He was in the early stages of a project with a company with several negative Net Promoter Score (NPS) survey ratings (sent to customers to ask them how likely they are to recommend you). In Andrew's experience, a customer who gives a poor NPS *and* specifically cites an issue wants a dialogue—they are not wasting their time to trash you; they want you to reach out. They divided these customers up for each of the executives to reach out to, including the head of engineering and the head of product. In response to this strategy, the CEO said, "I don't want my head of engineering and head of product to waste their time talking to customers." That is not at all in the spirit of being curious and getting in the trenches to see a customer's perspective. It was at this point that Andrew parted ways with the client, unable to effectively help them evolve their customer-success organization because the CEO didn't buy into the premise of a customer-focused organization that empathized with their customers' challenges.

Ellen Petry Leanse, the former Apple user evangelist we met earlier, made this thinking a cornerstone of her work to better connect with Apple's core users. She says Steve Jobs was extremely adept at identifying patterns across all of the interactions he had through customer emails. He used those conversations to gain insight into what Apple customers longed for and what their aspirations were. His findings guided product ideation and business strategy. He refused to hold himself far above his customers, choosing instead to get in the trenches by screening individual user feedback.

"When we are too comfortable with the people we're connecting with, we get into a 'me too' syndrome. We're in an echo chamber," Leanse says. "Only by getting with people who actually cause our eyes to open a little wider and go,

'I never thought of it that way,' can we really expand our capacity for empathy and open our minds to design products better than we otherwise could."

Lisa Reynolds of CHRISTUS Health agrees. "An empathetic leader sees the associate as more than someone to get the work done," she says. "They understand the whole person and care about the whole life. They involve associates in decision making. If they sense something's not going right, they'll ask questions—not just assume an answer."

As a leader, you don't have to don a disguise and go full-on undercover boss, but it can help to try another job to see what things are like for your team or customers. Take a day or a week for investigative journalism: work the customer support phones, go on a sales call, visit a customer site to see how they use your products, or take on your administrative assistant's task list. (Just don't mess up the company holiday party or your colleague's travel arrangements.) Get creative! What you never want to do as a leader is deem those experiences "beneath you" or believe that customer interactions are a waste of time.

7. Find Common Ground

Although empathy is often described as the ability to imagine yourself in someone else's circumstances, it also extends to understanding where your circumstances overlap. Empathetic leaders embrace this philosophy and live it by finding common ground with colleagues, employees, and customers alike.

Entrepreneur and yoga teacher Anna Guest-Jelley has seen firsthand how focusing on shared experiences is essential to launching an empathetic business. She'd practiced yoga for more than ten years and was always the biggest person in the room. A chronic dieter, she once tallied that she'd tried sixty-five different diets throughout her life. "I thought, *I don't need a sixty-sixth diet. What I need is a different relationship with my body.*"

With that realization, Guest-Jelley started on a journey of learning more about body acceptance: going to therapy, reading books, and continuing her yoga practice. "I had this moment," she says, "where I thought, *It's not my body that's the problem. It's that my teachers just don't know how to* teach *bodies like mine.*" Guest-Jelley recognized that because she didn't have a "typical" figure for yoga, her instructors got stuck. All they could see was how different she looked, so they couldn't imagine how she experienced yoga. This epiphany spurred Anna to enroll in yoga instructor training. She wasn't looking to start a business, but she felt a strong need to share this information with others like her, because she had been looking for it for such a long time.

Guest-Jelley started blogging and then teaching for fun. First a local and then a national community started building around her work, all eager to learn from her. That's how, in 2011, Curvy Yoga grew into a booming business. The company now includes online classes for yoga practitioners, a network of body-positive yoga teachers, a popular blog, a podcast, DVDs, and a book, *Curvy Yoga: Love Yourself & Your Body a Little More Each Day.* Guest-Jelley also runs retreats and continues to train and certify yoga teachers in methods that are grounded in diversity, acceptance, and empathy.

"Yoga teacher training is usually geared toward bodies that are already thin, flexible, and able, but the vast majority of people don't live in those bodies," she explains. "I understand. I am in one of those curvy bodies! So, I teach yoga instructors how to orient themselves to body acceptance." Guest-Jelley focuses on finding overlap and common ground, showing the teachers she trains that even if they're slim themselves, they need to find ways to relate to other body shapes and types.

Empathizing with different sizes and ages and focusing on the common ground that all yoga lovers share helps students feel accepted and comfortable, which helps them learn. By emphasizing where experiences, abilities, and needs intersect, yoga teachers create welcoming learning environments. By highlighting the overlap, yoga teachers broadcast empathy.

"I feel like empathy is, in a lot of ways, about listening and hearing what is going on for someone else, rather than from the standpoint of 'Here's what I think you're going through,'" Guest-Jelley says. "In my business, that's such a huge part of it—listening to people's experiences, to their stories, and drawing patterns from that."

And she's well aware that while she can relate to many of her students, she, too, has to practice empathy for others. "I know that just because I live in a curvy body, I don't have the same experience as everyone else. We all have our own perspectives." Guest-Jelley created her business from a place of empathy, and now that business is cultivating empathy in yoga teachers across the globe.

Linda J. Popky, founder of Leverage2 Market Associates and author of *Marketing above the Noise: Achieve Strategic Advantage with Marketing That Matters*, is a strategic marketing expert and coach who helps organizations and leaders stand out in crowded markets. She also leads one of the premier global organizations for independent consultants. Popky encourages clients to find value in disagreement and helps them effectively navigate it. "Properly managed, friction can lead to out-of-the-box thinking and innovation," she says, "as long as you stay focused on the process rather than attacking individuals who hold divergent positions."

Ready to embrace, not avoid, disagreement and find common ground with your own colleagues, direct reports, and customers? Here are some actions you can take.

- **Find and articulate the higher order principles that g[?]
  both of you.** "Do this even if they seem extremely broad,"
  says Popky, "such as 'We both want to make the company a
  success' or 'We both want to serve the customer and make
  sure they come back again.'" Be clear that your intention
  is to work together to find a solution that *both* of you find
  acceptable.

- **Focus on areas where you both agree, even if they seem
  small or insignificant.** This helps you each move away
  from polarizing, binary thinking and into a mindset that is
  more about where you each stand on a spectrum. With a
  spectrum, you can each take steps to move closer together,
  but if there's a valley you can't cross, you'll never find your
  way to each other.

- **Get to their core truth.** Someone may be advocating a specific solution you don't agree with, but *why*? What is their
  real intent? If they want to slash the budget and you don't,
  perhaps their core truth is a commitment to fiscal responsibility. If you ask enough questions to get to their core
  truth, you can then have a productive conversation and
  work toward mutually beneficial solutions. "What you've
  got to find is what I call their core truth and what's behind
  their position or ask. If you want to find common ground,
  you have to make peace with uncertainty and be proactive about getting to the other person's core truth, which
  is usually what is driving their position," says Lisa Earle
  McLeod, the sales leadership consultant you met earlier.
  "You've got to differentiate between the two if you hope to
  find a suitable solution you are both happy with."

- **Use different language.** Ask, "What is your *intent*?" Words
  matter. Intent helps you discover the deeper motive.

McLeod finds this to a more disarming question than "What is your *goal*?" because it makes someone more fully explain their thinking, why they are doing this, and what they want.

- **Help each other save face.** If your colleague has gone out on a limb, find a way for them to come back toward the center without losing face. That means you should be prepared to give up small wins to achieve a larger objective.

- **Don't try to squelch disagreement.** Groupthink is often the worst possible outcome. According to Popky, organizational friction may make people uncomfortable but, if managed properly, can lead to innovation. The key is to encourage groups to raise issues, discuss the merits and challenges of each alternative, then come to a resolution on how to move forward.

- **Assume good intent and withhold judgment.** Assume the other person has good intentions so you can enter into a conversation with an open mind. "It's important to understand the difference between judgment and discernment," advises McLeod. "When I'm making a judgment, good or bad, it means I'm being judgmental about you and attributing motive that might not be there." Making judgments means you are applying emotions to the other person's position. But discernment takes emotions out of it to look at what is really going on. "Discernment is more like a biologist looking at cells," says McLeod. "They wouldn't say, 'Well, why are you doing that?'"

- **Adopt a "Yes, and..." approach.** "Yes, but..." responses shut down conversations, says Popky. "Yes, and..." responses open the opportunity for productive discussions.

- **Check in.** Follow up with positive reinforcement to build a longer-term relationship.

Popky shares this final piece of advice: "Don't confuse empathy with an abdication of responsibility. Listen to what others have to say, make sure they feel heard and that you will take their input into consideration, but be clear that the final decision may not go their way."

> Download a free reference sheet of these empathetic leadership habits at www.theempathyedge.com/resources and keep it at your desk so you can put one into practice each day.

Empathetic Leaders Build Empathetic Cultures

Empathy in a business begins with one individual, whether leader or not, choosing to *act* with empathy. While it's absolutely essential that empathy starts at the individual level, it can't stop there. For companies to live out empathy in real and meaningful ways, it must become the fabric of organizational culture. Next, we'll explore the benefits of empathetic company cultures and then investigate ways to foster that type of culture in your own organization.

Sharpen Your Empathy Edge

Leadership can take many forms within an organization, and empathy can be expressed in many ways. Here are seven simple ways to train yourself to lead more empathetically.

1 **Practice Presence:** If you feel constantly scattered and preoccupied, you'll have no capacity to consider others' perspectives or think clearly. Ground yourself through a daily practice of meditation or silence—even five minutes. Avoid distractions. Don't multitask.

2 **Listen More, Stay Humble:** Empathetic leadership requires restraint when listening to people's experiences, stories, and perspectives and drawing patterns from that information, without offering advice. Stay humble, and adopt a servant leadership mindset.

3 **Be Curious:** Highly empathic people (HEPs) find other people more interesting than themselves and are eager to learn about lives and worldviews different from their own. Stay open to other possibilities.

4 **Explore with Your Imagination:** Consuming stories that offer diverse viewpoints is a great way to get inside the minds of others. Immerse yourself in films, documentaries, art, theater, music, or biographies made by people whose lives are very different from the one you lead.

5 **Cultivate Confidence:** Without a healthy store of self-confidence, it is much harder to be present, listen, and practice curiosity—when we're busy doubting ourselves and fretting over negative judgments, there's no energy left to empathize with other people. Tracking goals and celebrating progress along the way, keeping a high-five file, or finding an accountability partner to

give you an objective point of view are great ways to bolster your confidence.

6 **Get in the Trenches:** A leader should never deem any experience "beneath" them or customer interactions as a waste of time. Try a colleague's job, work the support phones, or go on a sales call.

7 **Find Common Ground:** Look for ways to connect with colleagues, employees, and customers alike. The place where experiences, abilities, and needs intersect offers a chance to come together and form a community.

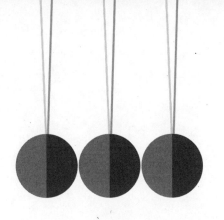

PART III

THE EMPATHETIC CULTURE

6

BENEFITS OF
EMPATHETIC CULTURES

Empathy takes time, and efficiency is for things, not people.
STEPHEN COVEY

AN ESSENTIAL COMPONENT of empathetic company culture is consistency: if your company's brand makes a promise to the market, your people must live out that promise. Otherwise, it's all just talk. If you say your company is innovative but you hire risk-averse individuals, that brand promise will never ring true. It's what I like to call "writing a brand check your company can't cash." A brand must be rooted in reality and what your organization can actually deliver. And who delivers on that promise?

Your employees.

They are the best brand assets you have. It's all well and good to invest in slick ads or groundbreaking marketing, but if your culture does not enable your people to practice what you preach in their daily interactions with each other and your customers, the brand facade will soon crumble.

Your internal culture must align with the external brand promise you want to convey in the market. Otherwise, the organization appears dishonest. You won't in any way be walking your brand talk, and audiences will soon figure that out. As Tony Hsieh, CEO of Zappos, has famously said, "Every employee can affect your company's brand, not just the frontline employees that are paid to talk to your customers."

Josh Levine is an author, speaker, and educator who evangelizes that company culture is a strategic business advantage. He runs a culture design consultancy called Great Mondays that advises companies on how to build strong cultures and employer brands and is author of *Great Mondays: How to Design a Company Culture Employees Love.* Levine is also the cofounder of CULTURE LABx, a collaborative community that curates conversations on the future of work. He has seen firsthand how culture can be one of a company's greatest competitive advantages.

"What's interesting and compelling about that is we've looked at competitive advantages previously like efficiency, quality assurance, design, and competition for talent, but those things don't necessarily benefit the employees. They benefit the business," says Levine. "A great culture, however, benefits the company, the customer, and, for the first time in business history, the employee. My work is about creating a system that supports employees in ways that enable them to make really good choices for themselves, the business, and the customer."

A big factor in creating that ideal internal culture is actively employing empathy to listen, understand, and collaborate effectively. Cultures driven by competition or ones that induce action through fear can never truly innovate. Employees spend so much time navigating cultural minefields that they have no bandwidth left for the things that matter: honestly surveying the market, customers, and opportunities to make crucial business decisions that drive the company forward.

Levine recalls one prospective client who refused to see value in gathering perspectives from other areas of the organization, saying, "We're not going to waste our time on any cross-functional tea parties." Such thinking does not create an innovative, market-leading, or empathetic culture. Not all the executives were that brutish but, unsurprisingly, the work Levine and his team did for the company in refreshing their values was essentially dead on arrival. Not because employees didn't buy in, but because senior leadership didn't believe the values applied to them. They only saw them as an HR tool for employees.

In Part II, we looked at how leaders can flex their empathy muscles. Now we expand that ripple effect to an entire internal team and organizational culture. Before we get to how to create this culture, let's unpack why an empathetic culture benefits the business.

Higher Retention, Less Turnover

Empathy is valued more than ever before by employees seeking a fulfilling work environment. According to the 2018 State of Workplace Empathy study by Businessolver, a software as a service (SaaS)–based benefits administration technology and services provider for HR professionals, 96 percent of employees consider it important for their employers to demonstrate empathy—a 4 percent increase since 2017. Despite this clear message from workers, 92 percent believe empathy remains undervalued by companies, a 7-percentage point rise since the previous year. In a tight labor market where competition for the best-skilled candidates is fierce, companies that fail to genuinely exhibit empathy and employ actionable policies that show they are committed to compassionate action will experience higher turnover and struggle to attract top talent.

Each of the three years in the Businessolver study history reveals that large percentages of employees would be willing to work longer hours for an empathetic employer. In 2018, that number was as high as 81 percent. And, according to Businessolver, more than two-thirds of employees in tech, healthcare, and financial services industries reported they would be willing to make tradeoffs on pay if it meant working for an empathetic employer.

"We've not only seen the benefits of empathy within our own culture," says Rae Shanahan, chief strategy officer for Businessolver, "but we've seen many of our clients who embody empathetic practices on a behavioral, leadership, and cultural level achieve success. We find that empathy is often a missed business opportunity, and we help our clients and other organizations realize how much it can impact their organization's innovation, productivity, and profit. Empathy can drive more collaboration and engagement across organizations while reducing costs associated with employee turnover." Basically, empathetic cultures make good, talented people want to stay and work hard.

In an article for the *Harvard Business Review*, Belinda Parmar of The Empathy Business writes that in her firm's own work with clients, they "found a correlation as high as 80 percent between departments with higher empathy and those with high performers."

High-performing professionals need to be acknowledged and rewarded in the ways that feel relevant to them. An empathetic culture will help them feel heard and understood and will be more proactive in finding the right ways to reward and engage them as individuals. Without that type of culture, the company may treat everyone in a cookie-cutter fashion, resulting in top people leaving for greener pastures.

If the best managers and team members express empathy and a willingness to act compassionately toward others, it stands to reason that companies with cultures that encourage empathy would attract highly engaged individuals. And that's what the data show. Empathetic companies have better retention, less turnover, higher engagement, and higher morale among employees.

The State of Workplace Empathy study respondents said that empathy motivates workers and increases productivity. Employees notice and appreciate an empathetic work environment and the organizations that value and exhibit empathy. So much so that 90 percent of employees said they would be more likely to stay with an empathetic organization, and 60 percent of employees said they would take a pay cut to work for an empathetic organization. Compare that to eight in ten employees who said in the survey that they would leave their current company if it became less empathetic. Organizations that have trouble demonstrating empathy face lower employee morale, higher employee turnover, and potentially business loss.

More Productivity and Financial Gain

Lisa Reynolds of CHRISTUS Health is quick to point out that linking empathetic culture and low profits is a mistake, saying, "Even in companies that are for-profit and make a lot of money, individuals can still show care and empathy and concern. Some of it is probably how that individual is just wired, but some of it is the culture in the organization."

There is ample evidence that an empathetic organizational culture can lead to bottom-line benefits. The 2018 State of Workplace Empathy study by Businessolver, mentioned above, found that "CEOs overwhelmingly link financial performance to empathy in the workplace." However, there is still a gap in the perception of empathy between leaders and employees. For example, while 90 percent of CEOs say their organizations are empathetic, only 78 percent of employees would rate their employer as such.

Leaders who make empathy part of their business have reported better performance from their employees and better overall business health. The study revealed that 87 percent of CEOs see a direct link between empathy and business performance. Forty-two percent believe that empathy has the potential to drive faster business growth, and 50 percent think more empathetic companies make more innovative products and services for customers.

And the numbers show empathy's value to an organization's bottom line. In fact, a more empathetic, engaged workforce could reduce absenteeism by more than 40 percent, increase productivity by 17 percent, and decrease turnover by 24 percent. As the saying goes, happy employees equal happy customers. More employee engagement has the potential to boost customer ratings by 10 percent and sales by 20 percent, because your employees want to work and are passionate and motivated by what they do every day. Embedding empathy into the culture and environment of your organization has the power to unlock untapped employee engagement and performance, which impacts business in a positive way.

Through multiple years of tracking empathy indexes at top companies, we can actually see evidence of financial gain, year over year. Belinda Parmar's published Global Empathy Index in *Harvard Business Review* found that the top ten empathetic companies that made the list in 2015 increased in value more than twice as much as the bottom ten and generated 50 percent more earnings defined by market capitalization from the previous year.

And empathy can help cut costs, too. The medical profession provides the most dramatic proof of how empathy can save a company money. Empathetic doctors can avoid expensive malpractice suits when things go wrong. One study shows that doctors who exhibit more empathy in their patient interactions decrease the chances of being involved in malpractice litigation and increase patient satisfaction scores. Those increased satisfaction scores can, in turn, lead to future business and revenue.

What does all of this mean to your particular business? Encouraging an empathetic culture in any organizational environment can save the company from angry customers who might sue but also can lead to happy customers who leave good reviews, refer their friends, bring repeat business, and build customer lifetime value for the company.

Let's look more closely at strong referrals. If you want to see repeat customers and customers transformed into super fans, make sure this empathy mindset enlivens the culture of your entire organization and everyone in it—from customer service rep to accounting managers. We'll talk more about the important role of empathy in word-of-mouth marketing in chapter 8.

One industry where empathy clearly counts is the ultra-competitive airline industry. Any company that can make flying more convenient and pleasant scores points with perpetually frustrated passengers. We've already discussed the string of PR blunders from United Airlines, which demonstrates the failure of empathy on its corporate level. But you may be less familiar with Ryanair's empathy success. After implementing their "Always Getting Better" program, which eliminated many customer annoyances like hidden charges, unallocated seating, and carry-on baggage restrictions, Ryanair saw a net profit increase from €867 million to €1.24 billion (US$1.39 billion). CEO Michael O'Leary famously remarked, "If I'd only known being nice to customers was going to work so well, I'd have started many years ago."

Who knew being nice could be so profitable?

Better Customer Service

Quality customer service has an input and an output. We'll address the output—how your public-facing customer service reps can treat customers with empathy—in Part IV when we dive into brand tactics. Here we're looking at the input: how the internal treatment of customer service reps by companies with empathetic cultures impacts their performance.

In many cases, customer service is a grind. These employees handle crises, put out fires, and resolve thorny issues day in and day out. If they get an earful from irate customers whenever they pick up the phone and an earful from tone-deaf supervisors whenever they hang up the phone, they are stuck in a cycle of negativity. They have no reason to treat the customers with respect because they aren't getting any respect themselves.

If, on the other hand, the company culture is supportive and solution-focused, that gives customer service workers the encouragement they need to reflect empathy toward the customers they serve. When they feel listened to, valued, and inspired by fellow employees and company values, they're empowered to pass that along.

In chapter 1, you read what happened to customer experiences when Christina Harbridge created an empathetic culture for her collection agency. When her employees felt understood and valued for the difficult and emotional work they did every day, they in turn treated customers better—and collection success rates soared.

Treat your customer service reps with empathy, and they'll work harder and more passionately on behalf of the organization.

CONVINCED THAT INFUSING empathetic mindsets and compassionate actions into the fabric of your culture will yield stellar results? Fabulous! Let's move on to tactics you can adopt to make your own company culture more empathetic.

Sharpen Your Empathy Edge

- Your employees are the best brand assets you have.
- If your culture does not enable your people to practice what you preach in their daily interactions with each other and your customers, the brand facade will soon crumble.
- Your internal culture must align with the external brand promise you want to convey in the market.

Here are some benefits of an empathetic culture.

- **Higher retention, less turnover:** In a tight labor market where competition for the best-skilled candidates is fierce, companies that fail to genuinely exhibit empathy and employ actionable policies that show they are committed to compassionate action will experience higher turnover and struggle to attract top talent. Empathetic cultures make good, talented people want to stay longer and work harder. Organizations that have trouble demonstrating empathy face lower employee morale, reduced retention, and potentially business loss.
- **More productivity and financial gain:** Happy employees lead to happy customers. Some studies suggest that CEOs link financial performance to empathetic environments. Leaders who make empathy part of their business have reported better performance from their employees and better overall business health. One study finds that a more empathetic, engaged workforce could reduce absenteeism, increase productivity, and decrease turnover by significant percentages. Encouraging an empathetic culture in any organizational environment can save

the company from angry customers who might sue but also can lead to happy customers who leave good reviews, refer their friends, bring repeat business, and build customer lifetime value for the company.

- **Better customer service:** Here again, happy employees equal happy customers. If the company culture is supportive and solution-focused, customer service workers are encouraged to reflect empathy toward the customers they serve. When they feel listened to, valued, and inspired by fellow employees and company values, they're empowered to pass those feelings along.

7

HABITS AND TRAITS OF EMPATHETIC CULTURES

How to Create an Empathetic
Environment Where Your
People Can Thrive

---

*People become motivated when you guide them to the source of
their own power and when you make heroes out of employees
who personify what you want to see in the organization.*

ANITA RODDICK, FOUNDER OF THE BODY SHOP

ET'S CIRCLE BACK to Lisa Reynolds, vice-president of talent management for CHRISTUS Health. Compassion has long been a core value for the organization, and Reynolds partners with hiring teams to bring on and develop people who operate from a place of empathy, love, and concern.

"It's just who they are," says Reynolds. "We look for that in our people and simply place them in a work environment where those traits will help them succeed. They make our culture more empathetic, not the other way around, and we want to hire those people to ensure we always put our patients first."

She shared a moving story about a CHRISTUS Health neonatal nurse named Melanie, someone whose innate empathy never goes off the clock—an ideal employee for the company.

"Melanie got a call saying that her mother was dying, so she had to go back home to the Philippines," Reynolds explains. "While she was there, her mother passed away. On the day of her mother's funeral, she was crossing the street to go into the chapel and she heard a commotion. She immediately recognized the noises as a woman in distress, going into labor in a pedicab."

Instead of heading into her own mother's funeral, Melanie immediately ran to the pedicab and helped to deliver the baby right there on the spot. Trained in neonatal care, she saw that both the mom and baby were in distress—the mom hemorrhaging, the baby blue in the face—and insisted that the pedicab driver get everyone to a lying-in center (akin to a physician clinic).

"The husband and Melanie take the mom and baby to the lying-in center, where the staff gets Mom stable," Reynolds continues. "Melanie gets the baby into an incubator right away because she knows what to do. The baby begins breathing and she makes sure everybody's stable before she goes back to her mom's funeral, already in progress."

Are you teary yet? Hang tight, because Melanie's not done being amazing.

"After the funeral, she's thinking about this family—when you go through something like that, you get close to them—and she found out this was their eighth child and they were very poor," Reynolds says. "So, she bought some clothes and supplies and took them back to the lying-in center to give them to the family. They placed the baby in her arms and told her they'd named her after Melanie's mother."

Melanie had the seeds of compassion inside her before she signed on at CHRISTUS Health, and her ability to see other perspectives and recognize needs meant she fit perfectly within the company's existing culture. But being hired and trained by an organization with empathy at its core enabled her to use her skills to save the lives of strangers in the midst of her own personal tragedy. CHRISTUS Health saw her potential, knew she would fit well into a culture driven by care and concern, and nurtured her abilities. It's a beautiful kind of symbiosis.

As you'll see, empathetic culture isn't just about rules and behaviors: it's about bringing in the right people and giving them what they need to thrive. With that in mind, here are six tactics for ingraining empathy in any corporate culture.

1. Start Small

Good news: you do *not* have to roll out a multi-million-dollar training initiative and spend years reconfiguring internal protocols! Sparking empathy within your culture can happen slowly through tiny, cumulative actions. Belinda Parmar calls these "empathy nudges."

"A lot of clients are used to these big transformational programs, and 70 percent of them fail because they're too time-consuming and too costly," she says. "The reason why the clients love the nudges is that they break empathy down into bite-sized, small things that build up to something bigger."

One of her firm's empathy nudges is language. For example, Belinda worked with a company that used the term "front-line" when describing the customer-facing component of its workforce. It's a term that has military origins and implies the first line of defense, meaning the grunts who take the majority of the flak. (Literally!) Belinda had the company start using the term "front of house" instead, and doing so helped raised the status of the employees who were dealing with customers every day.

In Parmar's work with a bank, she realized that many employees bristled when they heard the term "head office," since "head" implied superiority. Belinda suggested they switch to the term "support hub," which reinforced the idea that the people in the upper ranks were actually there to serve the other employees.

Both of these "empathy nudges" are simply tweaks in language, which may seem insignificant on the surface but can have a huge impact. Workplace terminology influences our perceptions of power, value, hierarchy, and respect. When we're intentional about the language we use, it imbues our workplaces with thoughtfulness and empathy.

Consider polling your employees about how departments or working groups are named. Do your workers feel insulted by internal nomenclature? (Comedian John Mulaney tells a story from his childhood that illustrates the importance of naming. His class was put into two groups for math class: the math lovers were called the "Blue Angels," but the rest of the students, including him, made up "Group Two." Not exactly inspiring, right?)

If hierarchical naming doesn't seem to be an issue, start tracking the casual terminology used throughout your company. Perhaps the non-sports fans are sick of being told to "knock it out of the park" or prepare for a "full-court press." Maybe your employees don't want to be called "buddy" or "kiddo" or "hon." Be curious, find out what's chafing, and make changes at a company-wide level.

Here are some other small steps your culture can take to show empathy.

- Implement flexible work hours to accommodate working parents or caregivers.

- Conduct stand-up meetings that make better use of everyone's valuable time by focusing on the pressing issues—

blessedly avoiding interminable "status updates" that do no one any good.

- Designate a rest area or "alone time" space, especially if you have an open floorplan office, for introverts (or those with neurological issues) who get overwhelmed by too much outside stimuli. Many offices now offer these types of "telephone booths" or cozy nooks to help people with different needs do their best work.

- Provide a private nursing area for moms (no, a cramped ladies' room stall is not a great option). In some instances, this is actually required by law if you have such an employee, but be proactive and create the space. Use it as a meditation room when not required to help your leaders with the habits in chapter 5!

- The simplest small step of all: allow people to dress comfortably at work (within reason) and do away with any stodgy dress code requirements, if possible.

2. Create an Environment of Trust

When we don't feel safe, we put up barriers to ensure our own survival. We can't put our own needs aside, listen, and see other perspectives when we're too busy protecting ourselves. Empathetic cultures can flourish only if employees feel secure enough to stop looking over their shoulders or protecting their turf.

"Organizations just run a hell of a lot better when there's trust," says Cory Custer of Brighton Jones. Custer mentions Robert Kegan, developmental psychologist and author of *An Everyone Culture*. "He says everybody is running around all the time doing two jobs. One is their job-job, and their other job [is] trying to protect themselves, not look weak, look good, keep up their barriers. His premise is if you have the right culture of trust, then you can let go of all that stuff. My boss can give me feedback and I can give him feedback. He signs my paycheck, but we can have those conversations; we can take risks, we can help each other, and all the bottlenecks start to go away. I think we're seeing a level of collaboration and creativity that comes through innovation and risk-taking because people aren't afraid to try something and fail."

Just as leaders must work on themselves before they can inspire empathy in their employees, companies need to create the right internal conditions for empathy to thrive. You've got to "get your own house in order" before you can expect your workforce to fall in line. That starts with the organizational culture. Is it cutthroat and competitive? Is information treated as currency to be hidden, manipulated, or leveraged, or is there a free flow of ideas and perspectives? Are employees who go the extra mile rewarded with *more* work instead of praise, compensation, or rewards that actually matter to them? Take a look again at the Platinum Rule discussed in chapter 1.

Some fundamental ways to make an organizational environment safe include good leadership, supportive policies, mentorship and training, and open communication.

Strong leadership driven by empathy is essential to cultivating company-wide compassion, as we saw in Part II. Leaders must set the example, so others know it is safe to bring openness and compassion into their work. When leadership listens, asks questions, models curiosity, and strives to find common ground, employees understand that those traits are not just accepted but valued.

The next step is to create supportive policies and fair structures, so people can bring their authentic selves to work and ensure their jobs align with their own personal values.

Are they rewarded for taking risks, collaborating effecti
and generating new ideas without a fear of failure? Does the
culture encourage open and honest conversations without
harmful consequences, or does it tacitly imply everyone better get in line and not rock the boat?

A great way to kickstart this is to open every brainstorming
meeting with a set of ground rules that includes "*All* ideas are
welcome. No fear, no judgment." Leadership can reinforce
openness and creativity by praising employees who made stellar suggestions that didn't pan out: show the workforce that
"failure" is relative, and taking risks is safe.

In fact, how you run every meeting is a great playground
for encouraging trust. After all, most people want to poke their
eyes out when yet another meeting is suggested. So what can
you do to create a meeting that people *want* to attend? Kim
Bohr, executive advisor and CEO of The Innovare Group,
whom we met in chapter 5, suggests thinking through three
stages to make these conversations meaningful and bolster
trust.

- Stage 1: preparation
- Stage 2: meeting opening
- Stage 3: meeting management

"Preparing well for the meeting demonstrates respect and
empathy to the various learning and communication styles of
each person in the room," says Bohr. In order for your meetings to be productive and foster full participation, set time
aside to prepare (Stage 1) in the following ways:

- Prepare a clear agenda, including a summary stating the
  meeting's focus, relevant resources or actions taken up to
  that point, why this topic is important, and how it aligns
  with larger team or company initiatives.

- Send the agenda out twenty-four hours ahead of time for those who need more time to process and prepare.

- State clearly on the agenda your expectations and interest for their participation.

For Stage 2, opening the meeting, Bohr advises that you take a moment to review the highlights of the agenda, drawing attention to the areas you believe need to be covered most thoroughly. Remind everyone how important it is to have each person in the room, as their expertise is valued. If the meeting is short or there are many attendees, consider setting a timeframe up front for each person to share their thoughts (for example, five minutes each). Finally, finish your opening remarks with a statement that reflects the goal of the meeting and the intent to move this important topic forward as a result of the time together.

Stage 3 is managing the meeting itself with empathy and inclusion. Bohr advises using these tips and phrases so each person feels seen and heard:

- "I'd like each of you to share your initial reaction (or thoughts) to what I've talked about so far." (Go around the room to each person.)

- When someone shares something that you may not agree with or need more clarity on, default to a curious mindset. Respond with "Please say more. I want to understand your perspective further."

- After you've asked for clarity, say "thank you." The quickest way to shut down a conversation is to respond defensively or in a way that gives the impression of dismissing someone's opinion.

- For those who are assigned tasks coming out of the meeting, make sure they have the support needed to deliver on these commitments. A great question is "Is there anything you can foresee getting in your way to accomplishing this?" Or "Are there any obstacles you are facing now that you need help removing in order to meet this deadline?"

- Send a status update in any follow-up communication in order to close the loop. People want to know what decisions were made and why their recommendations did or didn't fit—this shows that you heard their concerns and their opinions matter.

Cultivating strong mentorship and training programs within your culture also breeds trust. It shows that the organization cares about individual development and is committed to employee success. Informal mentorship is typically not enough. Mentors need proper guidance on how to be good mentors, and protégés need to understand their role and responsibility in the process. If your company doesn't offer a structured program, thoughtfully create one to illustrate that the company values cooperation, openness, ambition, and collaboration. Create a framework in which the program's goals are clear, both sides have input, and there is a continuous feedback and metrics loop—otherwise such a program can cause more harm than good.

Michelle Tillis Lederman, leadership speaker, connection creator, and author of *The Connector's Advantage: 7 Mindsets to Grow Your Influence and Impact*, offers these helpful tips:

- Before pairing people up, have participants get clear on what a successful mentor relationship looks like for both parties. This way, matchmaking can be based on shared objectives and expectations.

- Build both structure and flexibility into the program. Structure ensures a path to follow when both parties are unsure, but flexibility allows pairs to create a format that suits them best. For example, set up regular meetings but encourage participants to decide how to communicate or where to hold those meetings (in person or via video call). Recommend they get creative about incorporating social elements as they see fit, but in addition, include a few programmatic group social opportunities if possible.

- To be successful, both parties should be willing to share what they are working on and how they can help each other. Even those who think they have nothing to offer someone more experienced can often add great value; for example, a fresh-out-of-college new hire can help an executive navigate social media marketing. Mentorship provided in both directions offers the ultimate empathy exercise, as both people learn to see things from the other's point of view.

- Consider all aspects of the program—informal, formal, and social. Ask people how they would like to interact, as well-rounded connection creates a stronger bi-directional relationship.

3. Enable Open Communication

Creating an environment of trust is contingent on free-flowing, unfettered communication. Without barriers or facades, your people can feel confident that the company culture values their voices, feelings, and contributions.

Eric Dawson is CEO and founder of Peace First, a non-profit that provides a platform for young people around the world to become changemakers for social justice now, rather than waiting until they are grown. His organization believes no one has to wait to reach a certain age before making the world a better place. Despite their global reach and incredible success, his organization is still a non-profit: that means long hours, strapped resources, and a small staff performing heroic acts every day.

Dawson believes that Peace First's secret sauce to success has been creating a strong culture, rooted in empathy. "No matter what type of organization you run—for-profit or non-profit—I think culture is culture," he says. "When empathy is the root of how an organization conducts itself, especially internally, people are happier and thrive more in their performance. They feel cared for and attended to."

It would be easy to fall into the trap of believing that non-profits instantly cultivate empathetic cultures, since they tend to have noble, selfless missions. But Dawson confirms what I found to be true in my research: this is not always the case.

"There are a lot of organizations that have terrific missions and do terrific work but are not very nice places to work because of how they operate internally," he says. "I think 'do-gooder' organizations do a lot of damage to people, because they don't have the right level of internal empathy and compassion and care for the folks who work for them."

Dawson feels the key to creating a trusting environment where empathy can thrive is to encourage and generate open conversations. At Peace First, senior leadership gathers for a meeting every Monday morning. Instead of jumping into business, the first thing they do is to encourage everyone to take a minute or so and ground the group about where they are in their personal life.

"We don't problem solve, we don't manage it, we don't respond," says Dawson. "It's a chance to say, 'Here's where my project is and my mom's really sick and I'm having a hard time sleeping,' or 'My kid's being potty trained and I'm knee deep in crap, literally.' Then we take a breath together to just let that settle. I think what has been powerful for our team is that it's an invitation to wholeness."

Getting to know your coworkers on a personal level builds trust, and trust allows empathy to flourish. When your kid is sick, you don't stop worrying about that when your first meeting of the day starts. But when others can see and understand what you're dealing with, they can better adapt to your needs and understand your current mood, mindset, and motivations.

Creating trust in remote working environments is a whole different ball of wax. But, with a little creativity, you can create an environment that enables your people to feel empathy across the wires and miles, sometimes with folks they've never met in person.

Jay Baer runs a remote organization, Convince & Convert, a digital strategy consulting firm that helps prominent companies gain and keep more customers. His media division runs the world's number-one content marketing blog, multiple podcasts, and many other education resources for business owners and executives.

"We've got fifteen to twenty people spread out all over the world," says Baer. "Being a completely virtual organization requires proactive and strategic empathy at a high level, because you don't have the situational or atmospheric cues you have when people are all together. You can't necessarily walk by somebody's office and see them sobbing and think there's a problem that might need to be addressed. As more and more people do virtual work, it's increasingly important for managers to be purposefully empathetic, not just organically empathetic."

Baer says this takes time and an intentional strategy. How can you find opportunities to build that trust and hence empathy among those remote employees? One way that Baer has handled this is to schedule regular one-on-one video calls with his team, so he has a sense of what's really going on for them, good or bad. He takes the time to engage in their personal lives over the wires and doesn't rely on email communication alone, since it never creates that essential empathetic bond.

Here are five ideas for building stronger connections and encouraging empathy within a remote workforce.

1   **Leverage technology to stay connected.** Not solely video calling to see each other's faces, as Baer proposes, but also use collaboration tools such as Slack, Google Hangouts, Workplace by Facebook, Microsoft Teams, HipChat, or Stride where employees can easily collaborate for work... and play. Many companies use Slack for more than just work projects, often creating fun channels where employees can share favorite music, upcoming vacation plans, or celebrate each other's successes. (It helps eliminate the biggest downsides of working remotely: missing out on "good" office gossip, shared jokes, and "breaking" news!) Such tools bring everyone together and you can capture some of that shared camaraderie.

2   **Gather employees together in person.** When a remote employee is first hired, fly them to the home office to get to know their coworkers face to face. And where you are able, gather them together for in-person events on a regular basis, perhaps rotating through different cities. I once worked with remote team members; at least every two months, our boss flew them in to work with us for a few days. That personal interaction was invaluable to team chemistry and allowed us to get to know each other better. In one case, our entire team flew to our remote teammate outside of Chicago, and it was so helpful to see his work

environment, so we could better understand his point of view.

3 **Level the playing field.** I really love this one! When you have remote team members, use technology to create the same experience for everyone, so no one feels left out. An employee from Nomo FOMO, a travel app, shared this idea in a *Forbes* article: "When we do team-building calls, we have everyone in the same room be on their own computer and camera so that the remote employees don't feel left out. We all talk better together that way and no one gets preferential treatment."

4 **Switch up meeting times.** Your UK workmates will really appreciate if you don't start all team meetings at 1 p.m. Pacific time, which is 9 p.m. there. Nothing shows empathy more than if you are mindful of times and take turns getting up early or staying late. While working in San Francisco, I had colleagues in France and sometimes had to take one for the team and run a meeting at 7 a.m. my time, or 7 p.m. my time for Asia Pacific counterparts.

5 **Designate a Remote Worker of the Month.** Have some fun and choose one person working remotely who will educate (and entertain) the team by telling them all about where they live, maybe even taking them on a virtual tour of their town. This helps others get a glimpse into that person's world and perhaps have a better appreciation (and empathy) for the weather, traffic, or environment in which they work every day.

4. Facilitate Intergenerational Understanding

Empathy can go a long way toward breaking down the barriers of generational tension. Millennials are flooding the workforce, and we've all heard jokes about the classic tug-of-war between seasoned, experienced professionals and their upstart, entitled, distracted millennial team members. Those jokes are hurting more than they're helping.

In his work running Convince & Convert, Jay Baer works with hundreds of companies on how to improve their customer service and connections. "One of the most common fulcrums for empathy in modern business is generational understanding," he says. "It's such a key topic: understanding how millennials and even Gen Z workers prefer to be managed, and grasping how their worldview differs dramatically from their cohorts in Gen X and Gen Y. Managers need to vary how they interact with those team members and display situational empathy for their worldviews and their values."

Sitting down with individuals to uncover what truly motivates them to do their best work is the key to a more empathetic culture. What people look for in a job and what fires them up have evolved; what motivated *you* to do good work may not be what drives someone else. For many millennials, for example, the driving factors for job satisfaction are autonomy, impact, more time off, and recognition—not merely an increase in pay or a fancy title. The entire culture must be set up to facilitate these conversations and adapt to differing incentives.

A more empathetic culture can dissolve many generational misunderstandings and misconceptions. Encourage open dialogue, create senior and junior mentoring relationships, or perhaps even be more direct and host a generational salon every month where people represent teams of different generations and can joke and openly discuss the stereotypes and assumptions they see the other groups having. This could be led by a deft facilitator who can spark conversation and unearth real feelings, without allowing the gathering to turn ugly or morph into a workplace violation!

5. Leverage Accountability and Rewards

Creating a culture where empathy is not merely lip service requires behaviors to change. And in a working environment, nothing does this better than accountability and rewards.

If cutthroat competition is rewarded—a "win at any cost" mentality—that's the MO that employees will adopt to get ahead. If risk-taking and innovation are the keys to a plum new assignment, promotion, or praise at the next company meeting, workers will slow down and spend the time to invent creative solutions.

In other words, you get the culture you reward.

If you tout empathy and compassion as important but punish workers for missing goals even if they do the right thing, this sends the wrong message. You have to be prepared to accept some missteps along the way if you want to encourage empathetic behavior long term. Likewise, are you only promoting people who exceed their goals at any cost, over those who might miss a quarterly objective to spend more time going above and beyond helping a customer or colleague in trouble? No matter what you might say, employees notice such contradictions in behavior and will act accordingly. Actions speak louder than words.

Next Jump, a technology company that provides a company perks platform as well as a suite of HR tools, helps their clients build developmental, adaptive cultures. In fact, Next

Jump was included in the book *An Everyone Culture: Becoming a Deliberately Developmental Organization*, where a team of Harvard professors cited the company as one of three Deliberately Developmental Organizations, or DDO, which represent the future of work.

Next Jump clearly knows a thing or two about creating winning cultures. And they base everything they do on their core values, one of which is humility. They issue an annual Avengers Award to the person voted by their peers to help others the most, by however they define it: "The Avengers Award is focused on the trait of 'service for others' and recognizes the Next Jumper who most exemplifies steward-leadership. The ideal candidate is someone who creates an environment that helps others succeed by caring for and serving those around them, someone who is always helping others and putting the group before self. It is an annual peer-nominated award at Next Jump."

Folks are nominated throughout the year, generating excitement and recognition for their helpful ways, and the top ten are called out every month. Then those people go on to a peer selection committee. And what does the annual winner of the Avenger Award receive? A paid vacation anywhere in the world for their entire family. In 2018, Next Jump went one step further by also rewarding the winner's Talking Partner, or the person who enabled that winner's success.

So, yes, they made the stakes very high. It shows commitment and that the company is not messing around when it says it values humility. This is how you energize your employees to adopt a particular mindset.

Kronos Incorporated, a leading provider of workforce management and human capital management cloud solutions, also knows how to reward employees for exhibiting the values they hold dear. CEO Aron Ain, who is also the author of

WorkInspired: How to Build an Organization Where Everyone Loves to Work, often tells employees that if work is the most important thing in their lives, they need to reevaluate their priorities. And he means it.

Part of this value system is to ensure employees remember that everyone on the team is a person with a life. As a family, the company values being there for each other and understanding when a colleague might have to take care of a sick child or deal with a family emergency. The company's performance evaluation captures such behaviors, and employees are rewarded for being there and stepping up for colleagues when needed. In 2019, Kronos was named one of the FORTUNE 100 Best Companies to Work For® by *Fortune* magazine and global research and consulting firm Great Place to Work®.

If you're rewarding and recognizing people who exemplify empathetic behaviors, other workers will equally take notice. Taking time to call out heroic acts of empathy in an all-hands or departmental meeting, adding empathy as a performance review criterium, and highlighting the empathetic actions of those who get promoted and succeed will tell a much more powerful story than proclaiming "We are empathetic" on a company poster.

Putting the right accountability structures and rewards programs in place—from evaluating new hires to promoting seasoned veterans—ensures you balance ambition, innovation, and healthy competition with empathy.

Ask these five questions of your organization to determine where measures can be put in place:

1 What questions or criteria do we use when hiring?
2 Which behaviors are rewarded, celebrated, and held up as examples?
3 How are people promoted?

4 How is their performance evaluated?

5 How are they recognized by their peers or managers?

If compassion is deemed important, people need to know that acting on it will impact their success and advancement within the organization.

6. Hire for the Culture You Want to Create

As we saw in Part II, empathy starts with the individual. It's about hiring right so your organization can be filled with people who embrace and model empathy. But can you screen for empathy? What should you look for? Who are the people who won't only succeed but thrive?

If your hiring process is not set up to attract and filter for empathy, you will never be able to bring in the right people to support the culture. Of course, you need to hire to each job's skills and requirements, but you also need to screen for company culture fit. A values-driven and culture-based expectation must be set with recruits so you attract the right candidates. Then it's up to you to carefully select people who will bring the right mindset to work every day.

Cory Custer at Brighton Jones puts it bluntly: "We tell our candidates, 'Don't show up to Brighton Jones if you're not interested in becoming a better person.' Our recruiter puts this front and center." This is alignment of the highest order as it relates to ensuring your future employees are a good fit with the organization's culture and values. (We'll dive into alignment of a different sort—rallying employees' organizational mission in chapter 9.)

Brighton Jones has a team of internal people who interview everyone who comes in to look specifically for culture fit, as well as emotional and social intelligence. Here are some of their go-to questions, which help assess a person's empathetic bent:

- What was your biggest failure or disappointment, and how did you get through it?
- What have you done (or what are you doing) to become a better person?
- What is one of the most difficult pieces of feedback you've ever received?

"We look for emotional self-regulation, we look for empathy and we look for compassion, and we know how to spot it," Custer explains. "We give people real-time feedback and look at how well they take that feedback. We see how vulnerable they are when we talk about challenges they've had and mistakes they've made. For us, all of these are good indicators of empathy."

Custer and the team give candidates on-the-spot feedback during the interview: "For example, we've told candidates that we think they're talking too much or they've missed the point of the question or we don't think they've prepared well—those sorts of things. We don't do it to mess with them. We do it if it's genuine feedback and it will serve them. That usually gives us a view as to how well they take feedback."

How can you incorporate similar tactics into your own hiring practices? Bring your HR and recruiting teams to the table when you're having discussions to refine the organizational brand. It may seem like branding is not their purview or like external marketing discussions are irrelevant to recruitment. But the hiring teams need to understand and embrace the external brand so they can attract and engage the right people who will live out that brand promise in their daily actions.

In my client work, I insist that HR team leaders be part of brand strategy and messaging projects. You can't develop an external promise without ensuring that your team brings in the right employees to fulfill it. Establish a clear recruiting and interviewing process that will proactively unearth empathy and not simply result in "Well, this person seems nice."

In addition, retool your interview questions to tease out empathy. Ask recruits to talk about a time they sought to understand a differing position. Ask them to relate a story of how they turned a work foe into a friend. Dig deeper with their references about how they interact with others in the team, how they listen, how they make decisions, and whether or not they seek input from others.

Hiring the right people to exemplify empathy, both inside and outside of the organization, requires looking up from the résumé to evaluate values and cultural fit. While you can train someone how to code, you can't easily teach them how to be a kinder person, a more collaborative workmate, or a better listener.

Since most companies undervalue empathetic culture, new employees might be surprised to find themselves in an environment that focuses on support, communication, accountability, and understanding.

"Many people come into the organization from a variety of cultures, and it is a bit of a culture shock to come to a place where everybody smiles and says 'good morning' to you and appreciates the diversity in our work population," says Dave Ballai, the technology leader at Reed Tech you met earlier. "We have a very strong focus on women, on ethnic minorities, and we have a very large population that come from all kinds of backgrounds. We support an understanding of people of different cultures and experiences that you might not have had before. Our employees are very tolerant of one another and very supportive of one another."

A united, synergetic, harmonious workforce. And all it takes to cultivate that is a focus on empathy.

Now that we've explored the importance of empathetic leadership and organizational culture—the internal work to build a genuine foundation—we'll dive deep into empathy's value as an external brand attribute. Empathetic cultures breed empathetic brands, which will broadcast compassion to your customers and ensure your company is known for its generosity, flexibility, and open-mindedness.

Sharpen Your Empathy Edge

Empathetic culture isn't just about rules and behaviors; it's about bringing in the right people and giving them what they need to thrive. Here are six tactics for ingraining empathy in any corporate culture.

1 **Start small:** No need to tackle big transformation projects. Sparking empathy within your culture can happen slowly through tiny, cumulative actions.

2 **Create an environment of trust:** Empathetic cultures can flourish only if employees feel secure enough to stop looking over their shoulders or protecting their turf. Create a plan for meetings that enables everyone to safely contribute. Cultivating strong mentorship and training programs within your culture also breeds trust.

3 **Enable open communication:** Creating an environment of trust is contingent on free-flowing, unfettered communication. Without barriers or facades, your people can feel confident that the company culture values their voices, feelings, and contributions. Adopt strategies and leverage technology to create trust within remote working environments.

4   **Facilitate intergenerational understanding:** Generations have different expectations, desires, and motivators. Learning what truly motivates individuals to do their best work is the key to a more empathetic culture. Understand that younger generations expect their contributions to be valued and have been raised to believe that diversity of thought leads to better business outcomes.

5   **Leverage accountability and rewards:** You get the culture you endorse. Putting the right accountability structures and rewards programs in place—from evaluating new hires to promoting seasoned veterans—ensures you balance ambition, innovation, and healthy competition with empathy.

6   **Hire for the culture you want to create:** If your hiring process is not set up to attract and filter for empathy, you will never be able to bring in those who support the culture. Look for signs of emotional intelligence. Retool your interview questions to tease out empathy. Ask recruits to relate a story of how they turned a work foe into a friend. Dig deeper with their references about how they interact with others.

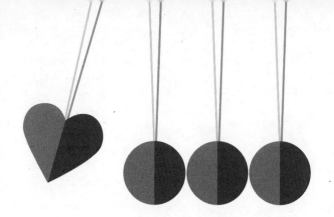

PART IV

THE EMPATHETIC BRAND

8

BENEFITS OF EMPATHETIC BRANDS

---

*I believe it's more than just doing the right
thing for a customer. It is doing the right thing
with empathy, sympathy, concern, and care.*

SHEP HYKEN, CUSTOMER SERVICE
AND EXPERIENCE EXPERT

BRAND IS REALLY the distillation of business performance. Your company's brand is its heart and soul, the essence of its mission and the core of its conduct. Empathetic leadership, empathetic culture, and empathetic branding build on and feed off each other. As senior technology leader Dave Ballai puts it, "They tend to be wrapped up as a package. You can't do something in isolation and expect to be called an empathetic organization." How a company is led from the top and the culture that supports its employees influence the public impression of the overall brand. A strong brand in the market starts from the inside out, not the other way around.

What Makes a Brand Empathetic?

A brand is the impression that people have of an organization, including both its reputation and public perception. This impression is created based on what the company communicates visually, verbally, and experientially.

In my work as a brand strategist, I educate organizations of all types—from the smallest businesses to non-profit organizations to midsized fast-growth companies—on branding, including reminders that you can't simply create a cool logo or a slick website and—voilà! —your brand work is done. Brand is your core, your essence as an organization, and it is conveyed in three important ways.

1 **Visually:** How you look.
   Design, colors, logo, font, layout.

2 **Verbally:** How you sound or read.
   Elevator pitch, website copy, voice, and tone.

3 **Experientially:** How you act and what it's like to do business with you.
   Your processes, people, quality, delivery. These will be vetted against the visual and verbal promise that you made to the customer.

All three methods have one thing in common: they are determined through a thousand different actions and decisions made by *people*. In other words, you can't have an empathetic brand unless there are empathetic employees driving it.

Jay Baer puts it best: "I don't think there is such a thing as an empathetic brand; I think there are brands that are staffed with a higher percentage of empathetic people and therefore it may feel like that brand in and of itself has a greater degree of empathy, but I think that's just a reflection on the collection of people."

In other words, you can have great values but display poor empathy.

Do we give up? Do we throw up our hands and say there is no way to be an empathetic brand? Not at all.

The secret to effective branding is taking the time to articulate who you are as an organization, who you serve, what value you offer, and how you want to show up in the world. All of these decisions are based on your organization's actual strengths: its authentic self.

Over and over again, I find myself in conversations with senior executives about how they want to be perceived in the market—what they want people to say about them. At times, their desires are wrapped up in ego or competitive jealousy ("We want to be just like Apple, because we want that kind of loyalty and success").

Talking about the brand you want is easy; acting upon it is the hard part. It doesn't matter if your brand ambition is to be seen as innovative, safe, edgy, disruptive, luxurious, transparent... or empathetic. No amount of advertising or cool design can make your desired position believable if it's not supported by reality. Where's your proof? You have to put the right processes and structures in place, hire the right people, invest in the right things, and reward the right behaviors so that what your customers experience is what you promise them through your brand marketing.

The good news: you can control all of that with intention. You can shape the inside to support what you want to say on the outside.

So, what makes a brand empathetic? Here's one set of measures to consider. Earlier, you met Belinda Parmar, founder of The Empathy Business, which measures and manages empathy levels in organizations. Her firm has codified these factors in order to create its yearly index of the world's most empathetic companies.

"My definition of empathy is the emotional impact that a company has on its people: its staff, customers, and society," says Parmar. When Parmar and her team consult with clients, they break empathy down into seven core factors that can be measured, captured in the acronym EMBRACE:

E empowerment
M meaning and purpose
B belonging
R reassurance
A authenticity
C collaboration
E ethics

Parmar's company uses its own proprietary tools and assessments to measure each of these seven factors. For example, to gauge level of empowerment, they ask leaders, "Do your people feel that, when they go to work every day, they can make a difference or that they are in control of their own destiny?" For authenticity, employees are asked, "Is there a gap between how you see yourself at work versus at home? Can you bring your best self to work?" How interviewees respond helps Parmar and her team create a big-picture view of the company's empathetic potential.

Parmar feels that belonging is absolutely essential to most empathetic organizations. To find out if employees feel welcomed and accepted, she asks questions such as, "Do you feel you're a part of something? Do you feel that when you speak, your voice is heard and that you matter?"

The fact that she's been able to so succinctly codify and capture the elements of a truly empathetic brand illustrates that empathy is an attribute that *can* be measured. Parmar's EMBRACE system provides companies with a framework for understanding if they're sincere or just blowing hot air.

If you feel like your organization is veering toward hot-air territory, here's a strategic shift to consider: customer-centric product design. Many organizations feel they've successfully "ticked the empathy box" if user-centered design (UCD) is part of their process. Are they right? Well, sort of. But the experience has to go beyond product development to exhibit a fully empathetic brand.

UCD has been a buzzy term in the tech world for years. This iterative design approach asks product designers to focus on users' needs in every single phase of the design process. UCD involves users throughout the design and build stages via a variety of research and design techniques, all of which help engineers create highly usable and accessible products.

Designers and programmers need to understand the users themselves, the tasks they need to complete, and the environments in which they'll be doing these tasks. The process aims to capture and address the whole user experience, not just isolated elements of it. In doing so, it forces product designers to think beyond the technology itself and consider how people will *use* the technology. Is the product easy to use and navigate? What resources are needed to address user concerns, skill gaps, and needs? This is where UCD dovetails into UX, or overall user experience. *User-centered design* is an intentional process that puts users at the center of everything and builds around them. *User experience* is the result of that intention. UCD => UX

Sounds like an empathy-driven practice, doesn't it? Perhaps for that reason, UX has expanded beyond technology or "product" design into services and other offerings related to a user's (or customer's) holistic experience. It has gained traction in industries as far reaching as housing, public transport design, and hospitality.

And yet many companies are still so focused on their proprietary strengths and existing offerings that they completely ignore what their customers want and need. They create their products around internal ideas that fail to reflect consumer demand and are shocked when these products fall flat.

If you don't believe me, ask the CEO of your cable company or most-used airline the last time they anonymously called customer support or flew in economy seating. They may be shocked at what the customer experience is *really* like.

If companies in the retail, healthcare, travel, and financial services sectors want to be seen as empathetic, they need to explore UCD, at least for a start. There's no better way to live out a brand message of compassion and care than to imagine your customer's experience and tailor your services to that experience. This technique shouldn't just fuel how our apps and software are created; it should drive what we're offered when we stay at a hotel or the investment options our financial planners show us.

Can a brand really be empathetic if it *doesn't* require UCD, if it doesn't adopt the user's point of view? Perhaps. But creating offerings with consumers at the center might be the quickest way to prove to them that you hear them, see them, and want to address their needs. This is one of the best ways to put words into action.

How will imbuing empathy in your brand give your company a market advantage? Read on to learn the benefits of building an authentically empathetic brand, from the inside out.

Healthy Market Performance and Longevity

Ensuring your brand is empathetic can lead to happier employees, bolstered revenue, and market longevity.

As we saw in chapter 2, one of the overall business advantages of empathy is increased sales and improved market performance. Since "brand" encompasses everything from logos to customer opinions, it's worth revisiting this idea.

In this context, we're looking beyond mere financials: market performance, as it relates to brand, encompasses things like longevity and adaptability. When your brand is genuinely empathetic, it means you can cultivate customer loyalty for the long haul and continually absorb new market segments. (Brands that lack empathy focus on exponential growth and huge profits but often burn out fast.) With empathy imbued in your messaging and culture, your organization is better able to hear and respond to customer desires, adapting and pivoting to fulfill their needs—all of which leads to bigger market share and tremendous staying power.

U.S.-based Nordstrom is one of the only department store chains that's endured with both physical and online presences. Why? Because they have always made it clear that they put customers first. And they have lived out this brand promise in the way they serve you in the store, right down to their generous return policies. Most people have heard the now famous story (and true, according to Nordstrom spokespeople) of a customer who tried to return a set of tires to an Alaskan Nordstrom location. He purchased them in the store that used to occupy the same space. As Nordstrom is an upscale retailer of clothing, shoes, and accessories, clearly the customer did not buy the tires there. But the Nordstrom manager made the refund anyway. While one hopes this is not common practice for the store's own profitability, the tale shows Nordstrom's more honest and loyal customers that its flexible return policy is designed to make their lives easier.

Seattle-based communication experts Fierce Conversations helped one of their clients implement an internal protocol that encouraged empathy. Leaders were asked to use a coaching conversation model with their teams that was designed to dig deep. It started with the simple question, "What's the most important thing we should be talking about?" This question allows the employee to drive the agenda and then gives the leader some follow-ups that encourage empathy-centric exploration. The questions probe deeper and deeper, allowing both leader and employee to home in on what's truly essential to the team.

"It is called the 'mineral rights model,'" says Fierce president Stacey Engle. "When you are drilling for water, you have to keep switching the bits out to dig further and further; the idea is you're getting to one layer, but you're asking more questions to get to another. In the case of our client Coast Capital, using this technique increased previous year monthly revenue by $425,000. Not only that, their employee engagement improved. Coaching scores improved by 23 percent." Engle adds, "There's a strength behind taking an empathetic approach that has revenue output to it."

Increased Customer Retention and Loyalty

Brands that brim with empathy on the inside have a much easier time cultivating customer loyalty with the public. Why? It's that inside-out concept again.

Internal leadership and culture both have a huge impact on external customer brand experience. They are the foundational elements that hold up the whole brand house. If call center reps are rewarded for doing the right thing—instead of being praised for taking the maximum number of calls per hour—customers are certainly going to have better experiences and thus a better brand impression. On the flip side, if workers are submerged in a culture ruled by fear and competition, they will treat customers accordingly, pushing those customers toward disappointing decisions, glossing over their concerns, and focusing on the speed of transactions instead of satisfaction. When the brand is empathetic, so are the employees, and that environment impacts the customer base.

Round Table Companies founder and CEO Corey Blake is acutely aware that empathy within a company leads to a favorable brand impression among customers. His organization works with writers, artists, and filmmakers to nurture and broadcast their ideas and stories, which means his clients are extremely attached to the work they do together.

"If we've got a client who has been triggered and they send an email that makes it clear something is going on, empathy gives me the ability to be graceful, not personalize their reaction, and recognize this probably has nothing to do with me," Blake says. "Now I can access not only my heart but also kindness in my response. I can meet that client where they are, help them feel heard, and then move to wherever they're desiring or needing to go. In the absence of empathy, I may collide and cause damage, I may alienate, I may lose a client, and they might walk away from an important project."

His insistence that *everyone* at Round Table Companies focus on personal connection and genuine compassion has earned him the loyalty of customers, including Zappos CEO Tony Hsieh, executive coach and bestselling author Marshall Goldsmith, and renowned psychology professor Robert Cialdini. And Blake has made sure that empathy reverberates throughout his brand: the company's tagline is "Vulnerability Is Sexy."

Forgiveness When You Fail (and You Will)

When your organization is lockstep with its customers and they feel like your brand is one that truly *gets* them, you become part of the fabric of their lives. When informed by empathy, the ongoing experiences they have with you encourage them to rely on, talk about, and repeatedly purchase from or support your brand.

Put another way, if customers feel like you have their backs, they will have yours.

When things go wrong and the brand slips up, there is brand goodwill banked that can withstand the misstep and allow customers to give you another chance. They will consider the experience an outlier, not the norm, especially if the actions the brand takes to recover from the incident convey even more empathy.

JetBlue has famously built its brand on making air travel easier, more fun, and more accessible. This is not just about advertising and messaging but extends to what they call "the product"—the physical experience of being on the airplane, including the seats, the lighting, the amenities, and the service. Unlike Ryanair's reactive approach to improving the customer experience, JetBlue proactively set out to discover what annoyed people the most about flying and made those things better: extra leg room, free TV, and eventually self-serve snack cabins that enable you to eat and drink anytime you're hungry or thirsty. "If you're not focused on the customer and making their experience better, I don't know what you're doing," said Jamie Perry, former vice-president of marketing at JetBlue. JetBlue consistently gets high marks from customers because the company offers low fares, excels at baggage handling, and never nickel-and-dimes.

In 2007, severe storms ripped through the northeastern United States, grounding planes and derailing travel plans for thousands of passengers. JetBlue, like every other airline, stranded passengers on the tarmac for hours while the Federal Aviation Administration figured out what to do, and this caused a PR nightmare for them.

How did the company respond? With its trademark transparency and customer focus. And consequently JetBlue's brand—and financials—rebounded from the hit. Even at the time, airline industry experts recognized that this resilience was because of the company's strong reputation for empathetic customer service. Many also credited the airline with quickly communicating a plan to compensate customers, knowing that folks were in the dark and needed information right away. As reported by Reuters,

> The carrier is paying out $10 million in refunds to passengers on canceled flights and issuing $16 million worth of vouchers to delayed passengers for future travel and has promised better communications with customers and improved procedures for dealing with delays and other difficulties.
>
> JetBlue apologized Wednesday in full-page newspaper advertisements in big markets, appealing to the flying public to give it another chance. "You deserved better—a lot better—from us last week and we let you down," JetBlue said.
>
> Its shares ended Wednesday up 2.3 percent to $13.19, above their $12.99 Feb. 13 close, before the ice storm.

JetBlue saw the situation through its customers' eyes and reacted accordingly. As a result of already brandishing an empathetic and helpful brand, customers forgave the airline. They realized these events were anomalies and not the standard experience upon which the company had built its reputation. Their customers already saw the airline as a key part of their lives.

Good Press and Word-of-Mouth Referrals

How you run your company can help you stand out and get more attention. And if you're seen as empathetic to the needs and desires of your customers, your brand can be unstoppable.

Acting with empathy can give your brand a visibility boost since customers will be inclined to talk about you more often. And the press loves covering stories of companies who break the mold and do something extraordinary.

REI, the U.S.-based retail and outdoor recreation services corporation (organized as a consumer cooperative), enjoyed loads of great free press when it implemented #OptOutside on Black Friday, the busiest shopping day of the year. The company took a huge risk when it decided to give employees a break by closing all stores and its online shop to let them spend the day with their families, while simultaneously encouraging customers to get outside instead of being trapped inside a crowded mall. That risk, born from the company's mandate and strong connection to its customers and employees, paid off with great press, exposure, and viral social media mentions that cost REI nothing from an advertising or PR perspective.

Nothing gets greater media coverage than when a brand reaches out in times of crisis. Airbnb offered free housing to evacuees of Hurricane Michael in Florida and Hurricane Florence in North Carolina, scoring the company big press hits nationwide and elevating brand perception among current and potential customers.

And customers love to go online and post positive reviews and social media mentions when a company empathizes with them and acts with compassion. In *Talk Triggers: The Complete Guide to Creating Customers with Word of Mouth*, Jay Baer and Daniel Lemin explain that using unexpected empathy to delight customers is one of five types of talk triggers, or ways to get people talking about your brand and referring their friends. The authors note, "In the zeal for efficiency and profits, most businesses simply will not invest the time to deliver empathy." When brands go the extra empathetic mile, people notice. They talk to their friends, and they give the brand a shout-out online or on social media that may be seen by millions.

All without the company paying a dime.

Baer and Lemin cite multiple statistics proving that this kind of word-of-mouth marketing can result in a multi-million-dollar savings on advertising, versus competitors who lack similar exposure.

Yogurt company Chobani makes news in outlets such as CNN and *Fast Company* because of how its founder's own refugee experience translates into empathetic corporate policy. The company employs hundreds of refugees, giving them opportunities to better their lives. *Fast Company* had this to say about founder and CEO Hamdi Ulukaya: "He has begun to forge a new kind of business leadership, one that fuses competitiveness with an unusually strong sense of compassion."

Could these moves all be viewed as a calculated attempt to create an empathy veneer? Perhaps. But I would argue that what makes these actions genuine in intent is how they are grounded in deep customer understanding or in personal experiences fueled by empathy.

So, how can you cultivate an empathetic brand and reputation? What actions, people, policies, communications, infrastructure, and training are required to ensure that your customers are happy and the company is doing well? In the next chapter, we'll explore strategies that will make your own brand more empathetic.

Sharpen Your Empathy Edge

- Brand is really the distillation of business performance. Your company's brand is its heart and soul, the essence of its mission, and the core of its conduct.
- A strong brand in the market starts from the inside out, not the other way around. You can't have an empathetic brand unless there are empathetic employees driving it.
- A brand is the impression that people have of an organization, including both its reputation and public perception—visually, verbally, and experientially.

Here are some benefits of empathetic brands.

- **Healthy market performance and longevity:** When your brand is genuinely empathetic, it means you can cultivate customer loyalty for the long haul and continually absorb new market segments.
- **Increased customer retention and loyalty:** Internal leadership and culture both have a huge impact on external customer brand experience. When the brand is empathetic, so are the employees, and that environment impacts the customer base.
- **Forgiveness when you fail (and you will):** When your organization is lockstep with its customers and they feel like your brand is one that truly *gets* them, you become part of the fabric of their lives. When things go wrong and the brand slips up, banked brand goodwill can withstand the misstep and allow customers to give you another chance.
- **Good press and word-of-mouth referrals:** Acting with empathy can give your brand a visibility boost since customers will be inclined to talk about you more often. And the press loves covering stories of companies who break the mold and do something extraordinary.

9

HABITS AND TRAITS OF EMPATHETIC BRANDS

How to Cultivate an Empathetic Reputation so Your Customers Adore You

---

Get closer than ever to your customers.
So close that you tell them what they need
well before they realize it themselves.

STEVE JOBS

LET'S DIVE RIGHT into the rituals, practices, and behaviors that your company can adopt to create an empathetic brand, no matter its size. The eight strategies that follow are designed to help you engage, connect with, and delight your customers on a continual basis, all while serving something more significant than your bottom line.

1. Align on Mission

Your brand has no hope of being perceived as empathetic—or innovative, helpful, or edgy, for that matter—if the entire organization is not aligned on one core mission. That core mission must inform every decision to ensure the organization is constantly seeing things through the customer's eyes. Because brand is more than just advertising and logos, it must be lived from the inside out. And the single best thread you can use to weave a cohesive brand impression is your organization's basic reason for being.

Your mission should not simply be a trite platitude only found on the website or a cute poster on the wall (that employees either resent or ignore). It needs to be crafted in such a way that it informs every action that employees take on a daily basis. Emphasizing compassion, humanity, and customer experience in the mission ensures your people can make the right decisions at every level, be they product decisions, promotional messaging, packaging options, or payment terms.

And while everyone in the organization must be aligned on mission, it's equally important to make sure your mission aligns with your customer's values. To build a truly empathetic brand, you must have respect for how your customers see the world, the challenges they face, and the goals they strive to achieve. For example, your company might have an underlying goal of "Make a boatload of money," but that goal isn't part of your mission. Your customers don't care if you make a boatload of money or not; they care how you treat them, what you offer them, and why you do it. That's why your mission statement has to align your people internally *and* ignite your customer base.

Consider JetBlue's story again. The company's original mission was "To bring humanity back to travel" but has been revised to simply "Inspiring humanity." This shift has informed the stellar customer service experience discussed earlier, and it guides everything from extra leg room to free TV to in-flight self-serve snack bars. This idea of democratizing a great experience means they don't spend all their time offering perks to 1 percent of their most lucrative frequent flyers. They give those perks to the masses and treat everyone with equal importance—and humanity. Without the entire company aligned around that mission of "Inspiring humanity," it would have a very different business model—and brand perception—indeed.

According to REI's executive vice-president and chief customer officer Ben Steele, "The mission and core of REI has always been to awaken and enable a lifelong love and stewardship of the outdoors." REI's #OptOutside campaign went beyond any marketing veneer. It proves what can happen when everyone is aligned on mission and when they empathize and listen to both customers and employees and share their values. The campaign paid off with loads of free press and social media mentions. The idea surfaced when Steele facilitated an internal workshop to reorient the company around brand and what that meant to REI's mission around the holidays.

Employees candidly discussed what the holidays personally represented to them, which contrasted with the reality of what the holidays have become in our culture: stressful, commercial, and focused on stuff rather than spending time with those we love in places we love. Days like Black Friday added unnecessary intensity and stress for members battling store crowds and for employees working that day. Someone tossed out, "We could never do it, but what if we closed on Black Friday?"

Steele responded, "Why couldn't we?" It was an electric moment. The team investigated how they could make this work and what it would mean to their, at the time, 12,000 employees.

"It was empathy for our employees first and our members second that led to this decision. We got so focused on this core idea, this idea to give people the day off to spend with people they love," says Steele. "And then invite the rest of the world and see what happens."

Because everyone at REI is so aligned on mission, Steele says the overwhelming response to taking this big risk was "Hell, yes!" "We had no idea if it would work," he says, "but that really didn't matter. If our employees knew what was most important to us, then that would be a win."

The company was blown away by the impact of #OptOutside. Other retailers joined in the campaign, as well as the U.S. state parks with a singular mission to reclaim the holiday. And it all started with empathy for employees and members.

"We had a pure intent that was inextricably linked to our purpose of encouraging people to enjoy the outdoors," says Steele, "but we also had people across the organization shepherding the idea so it could take root. We wanted to improve the experience of our employees and our community and it paid off."

C Space, a global customer agency, publishes an annual customer quotient (CQ) study that assesses what draws customers to certain brands. In 2016, the year after the first #OptOutside decision, REI was ranked the top CQ brand overall and the number-one company customers felt most respected by. A *Harvard Business Review* article from that same year points out, "Consumer mentions of the brand increased by 270 percent from 2015." And at the end of 2015, the co-op itself reported that revenues had increased by 9.3 percent to $2.4 billion, and digital sales were up 23 percent.

Steele reports that this bold move continues to pay off every year for REI. "I can tell you that nothing but goodness has come from the energy around #OptOutside," Steele told *GeekWire*. "We've got 17 million members, a million new members each year, massive growth in that membership base since that first year of #OptOutside. All that is good for the co-op and a thriving co-op community."

As C Space so eloquently puts it, "Customers trust companies that they feel understand them. They respect companies that they believe respect them in return. And the results of that reciprocity are evident in the CQ data and the bottom line."

2. Speak Your Customer's Language

Empathy starts with using the right language. Language can bring us together and make us feel united by purpose, or it can keep us at a distance, offend us, and polarize our views. And that means it's crucial to choose your brand's keywords, taglines, and other verbal keystones very carefully.

As we saw in chapter 7, Belinda Parmar works with clients on choosing the right language as a simple empathy nudge. Choosing the right words in the stories you write and the marketing you create can make or break your relationship with customers.

What are the right words? They are spoken in the language of your audience, what I like to call the Voice Inside Their Heads.

Words matter, so think about the most important and resonant words for your audience. Which words will make them feel alienated or condescended to? Which will make them feel valued, heard, and understood? Which words and phrases will show that you understand your customers, constituents, and community? What can you say that will endear your brand to them and make them feel understood, shouting, "Yes! This company totally gets me!"?

Choosing the right words is the start of the empathetic brand conversation. If you repel people with words, you've already lost the battle.

Although the language in marketing materials and sell copy requires careful consideration, empathetic brands also mind their p's and q's in more organic communications. In order to create an empathetic relationship between consumers and creators, Fair Anita, the fair-trade product enterprise, shares stories in both directions. With stories and pictures, it highlights the amazing artisan women creating the brand's products and talks openly about what they have been able to accomplish. But the company also makes a point of sharing customer stories with the artisans. Fair Anita is also very careful about the language they employ and intentionally strives to never paint the artisans as victims. Instead they're portrayed as leaders, activators, and changemakers.

Founder Joy McBrien works hard to avoid conflating sympathy with empathy. "We are conscious of the way we talk about the women we work with," she says. "We try to make sure we talk about women as actionable people in their own life stories, because they are. For example, I wrote a website story profiling Maritza, one of our artisans in Peru. She is severely physically disabled, which is quite obvious from her picture, but she's an incredible jewelry maker. She's living in this horrific circumstance but has taught herself to make jewelry and started selling in her local market in Peru. She wanted other physically disabled women or women who have children with physical disabilities to start learning with her. So when we talk about her, we use phrases like 'Maritza leads ten women in the creation of this jewelry.'"

McBrien and her staff work hard to use empowering, uplifting language when sharing stories from the company's contributing artisans. "I would never write a social media post that says, 'Buy this from my friend Kelsey in Minnesota because she's starving,'" McBrien explains. "If I wouldn't do that to her, why would I do that to a woman in Peru or India? We try to get rid of that pity lens, so a true empathy connection can emerge."

Reviewing language through the lens of your audience—regardless of whether this copy shows up on a rarely visited website page or in a national ad—is the key to ensuring a brand voice steeped in empathy. Such language makes your customer connections stronger, more emotional, and more enduring.

Wondering where to start? Here are a few suggestions.

- **The home and contact pages on your website:** Does the language here feel welcoming, compassionate, understanding? Does it immediately speak to what your customers want or need, so they trust that you can solve their problems or add value? If appropriate, can you find ways to add levity when talking to customers about their problems and complaints, thus humanizing the interaction?

- **Hiring materials:** Make sure your mission and company values come through loud and clear in any communications aimed at new hires or applicants. Let them know what they can expect from your company through the words you choose—and tap into what they care about when selecting their next employer. Bragging can be fun but remember they are evaluating if you're the right fit *for them*, too. Use language that puts them center stage.

- **Customer service scripts:** Review these with an eye for words and phrases that invoke blame, shame, or aggravation—or words that make employees sound like robots, rather than human beings. Your reps should be given words that reflect the brand's empathetic stance toward its customers. If possible, give your reps the latitude to customize responses on the fly for each individual case so the response is genuine.

3. Hire People Who Are Passionate about Customers

In chapter 7, we discussed the importance of hiring leaders and employees who show an innate capacity for empathy. Here, we're focusing specifically on external-facing roles, the folks who talk with and serve your customers directly. These workers have a special charge when it comes to empathy. While it's true that every employee should embrace and reflect empathy, the brand lives in the actions of the people who represent the company and help end-consumers get what they need. Especially in the age of Yelp reviews and social media backlash, one bad customer service experience can undo years of effort and millions of marketing dollars.

When I work with clients on their brand strategy, I insist they have a human resources or recruiting lead in the conversation. This demand is often met with confusion: what do those folks have to do with branding?

Everything.

Your brand must walk its talk, which means your people are your most important brand assets. And that means hiring the right brand ambassadors, people who can take the right actions and deliver the promised, expected experience.

No matter whether you are intentionally trying to build a "We care, we understand you, we're empathetic" brand or not, all customer interactions must be infused with empathy. If they're not, you risk losing sales and market share. There is no greater bottom-line reason to hire empathetic people than that.

To prove this, consider an online retailer that messed up my order. When I spoke with the customer service rep, she was frazzled and curt and had absolutely no empathy for my situation (I needed the item for a wedding I was flying off to the next day) and first blamed me for not filling out the form correctly. She then switched tactics and blamed the fact that the company was so busy handling other orders, it was not at fault for not responding to all my emails and implied I should be more understanding that they were understaffed, because they were getting "so many other orders." While I love the product, because of this interaction both by phone and email, I will not be buying from them again. And worse, I told my friends and complained on social media.

Companies can do a lot in preparing scripts that "show" empathy. They can give people the right language and decision trees, but customers can often see behind the curtain—and it can sometimes make them angrier if their problem is not handled correctly or with genuine heart.

Yes, empathy is innate to human beings, as we saw in chapter 1. But it can be taught or, as I prefer to term it, cultivated. Empathy is already there; it's just that some people may not have flexed that muscle very often or been taught to practice that skill. But let's call a spade a spade: it's much easier to hire people who are predisposed to being empathetic and acting with compassion. So, when you're hiring for customer-facing positions, how can you screen for empathy?

Sally Hogshead is an expert in fascination, as evidenced by her two *New York Times*–bestselling books, *Fascinate: How to Make Your Brand Impossible to Resist* and *How the World Sees You: Discover Your Highest Values through the Science of Fascination*. She's the CEO of How to Fascinate, a company that helps people uncover their highest value in work and life so that they can attract more clients and become more valuable in the areas that matter most. Through an in-depth questionnaire that reveals who you are among forty-two different personality archetypes, Hogshead's work reveals how the world sees you, rather than how you see the world. This insight helps you discover the tasks and roles for which you are best suited, your motivations, and your communication patterns. More than one million professionals, representing every archetype, have taken the Fascination Advantage assessment.

Based on her extensive research, she's found that people who are gifted talkers make ideal customer service reps. "If somebody is really good at using an engaging type of conversational style, it's going to be very easy for them to be at the front lines doing customer service and to be interacting with people all the time," says Hogshead.

Hogshead also advises asking questions or inquiring with references about whether a candidate is inclusive and enjoys working with other team members. Among folks who exhibit strong emotional intelligence, empathy markers include being considerate, attentive, and dedicated.

"Personalities who are analytical, methodical, and rational can seem less empathetic, because they're less likely to lower their barriers and share emotion with others," says Hogshead. "Empathy requires a certain degree of connection and sensitivity. Yet we all can apply empathy to strengthen bonds and build a greater connection with others."

If a rational, analytical person is made aware that they can have better success if they lower their own barriers and see what is going on with another person, they are often very willing to adapt. And if they are given step-by-step guidance on how to better see other perspectives and act with compassion, they will appreciate that even more than someone for whom empathy comes naturally.

Scripts and decision trees can help those with underdeveloped empathy muscles find the right words and actions, which can ultimately transform them from within. However, your company is much better served finding people who have situational awareness and can react on the fly—and giving them policy latitude to make an in-the-moment call. One can't possibly prepare an employee for every single quirky, unique, or emotional scenario they might encounter, but a flexible framework combined with hiring naturally empathetic people can go a long way. You can screen for this trait by asking about hypothetical situations when interviewing or even asking applicants to role-play. But to truly gauge their ability to improvise, you'll need to see them in action.

A story that has always stuck with me was one a woman shared in a management course I took years ago. She said she would be loyal to American Express for the rest of her life. When her husband passed away, she called to cancel his credit card. The customer service agent expressed his deepest sympathy and went above and beyond to help her deal with closing the account and ensuring everything was secure, as well as simply lending a sympathetic ear. The agent was so kind and genuine that she never forgot how the company (for, in her eyes, at that moment, he was the company) took care of her during a difficult time. No one scripted his reactions. This rep was simply given the right tools and authority by the company to take care of things from a policy perspective but also to act with empathy in the moment.

Marketing and customer service consultant Jay Baer shared an outstanding and personal example of "situational empathy" in action. "Last year my wife and I went to Australia," he told me. "We were in Detroit, making a connection to Los Angeles and then on to Sydney. We were on Delta, as I often am when I fly for business, and we're boarding first or nearly first. The gate agent scans my boarding pass, looks into the magic box, and says, 'Thank you, Mr. Baer, for being a diamond member. We appreciate your loyalty.' Then she looks at my wife's boarding pass, realizes that she has no status—she's barely silver and maybe not even that. In that moment, she figures out what this scenario is, does some mental calculations, looks my wife in the eye, and says, 'Mrs. Baer, I would like to thank you for all you do to allow your husband to spend so much time with us here on Delta. It appears as though he's gone quite a lot and that must be a burden on the family. I just want to say thank you from all of us.'"

"This was an absolute game changer," he went on. "And the thing about empathy is it requires you to have permission to make it up as you go along. There is no such thing as a successful empathy script."

He's hit the nail on the head: empathy in customer service is all about situational awareness. Those dealing with customers have to understand what is happening and why it's happening, then react accordingly. And, as Baer points out, they need to have the permission to do that. This is where empowering them with flexible policies comes in. You can tell when employees have permission to make things up as they're going along and respond genuinely from the heart.

You just can't script that kind of situational empathy. If you tried, it would never be authentic.

4. Implement the Right Customer Service Policies

Today's technology and emphasis on transparency mean frontline employees are now closer to the customer than ever. It also means these same employees should have the authority to address problems on the spot, based on each unique circumstance. This goes beyond a hiring issue and becomes a policy and process issue. How much do we empower our people to solve problems immediately and in ways that best serve our customers? And how much do those employees understand the customer's entire experience, their ultimate goals, and how all of that relates back to the company's mission?

In other words, does the customer service rep have a broader knowledge of the customer's needs beyond the one interaction they're having right now? Can they respond in a way that reflects what the company wants to achieve and how the company's mission is calibrated to support that customer? It all comes down to how process, technology, and policy align to support a customer service rep in adopting this holistic and, yes, empathetic view.

Josh Levine, cofounder of CULTURE LABx whom we met earlier, supports this view, saying, "If you understand what the benefit to the customer is, then you're going to have a deeper connection to the end goal and you're going to work harder to achieve it. As businesses scale, employees tend to get further away from the customer. That said, social media, and the Internet as a whole, has the power to shrink that distance. The web ensures that more customers understand what happens inside the once-opaque walls of corporations and can voice their support or displeasure directly. The same is true in the other direction: employees can connect with customers online to great benefit."

Many customer service policies exist to punish the outliers who are trying to fleece the company: those who don't pay their bills on time or who lie to get more than they deserve. Still other policies are designed to constrain your front-line agents, due to lack of trust or improper hiring. Such strict policies also make it easier to simply hire warm bodies, rather than invest in thoughtful screening and training. If you create a blanket policy that leaves no room for empathy "on the fly" but requires approval from three managers or ties every customer service rep's hands in the same way, you can better control costs and outcomes, right? Well, that's certainly the easy way. But you also leave a lot of angry customers (make that *former* customers) in your wake—who will then share their negative experience with other people.

Empathy in action requires more than just hiring "nice" people. Those people have to operate within systems, technology, and processes that enable them to serve a customer's need in the way that's best *for the customer in the moment.* It means putting policies in place that assume the best of your customers, so that those who are loyal don't feel like they are being constrained, inconvenienced, or punished. You have to be willing to accept the cost of a few bad apples if you want your good customers to perceive your brand as empathetic and understanding.

Amazon usually gets high customer service marks, despite its gigantic size and reach. That's mostly down to specific policies and processes put in place to create a seamless buying experience. The company understands why people might hate online shopping and addresses those concerns by removing all friction. From one-click purchasing to saving your shipping addresses to Amazon Prime's free two-day shipping, grocery delivery, streaming services, and free returns, they proactively remove every nuisance a customer might experience.

And while one would think that dealing with customer service for a company this size would be a nightmare, it's amazingly effortless. Speaking from personal experience, I have been able to contact someone immediately via phone, chat, or email or have them call me back within seconds. The reps are empowered to offer full refunds, future discounts, or free months of Prime service *in the moment.* No need to ask for approval, no need to connect me to another department.

You could say Amazon's reps are authorized to delight, and that is down to the policies the company has created. To support an empathetic brand, all companies should adopt customer service policies that enable empathy in every inter-action. No customer ever wants to hear, "I don't have the authority to make this right" or "We know it's inconvenient for you, but that is our policy and I can't change it in the system." Or the worst excuse I ever heard, in our technologically advanced age, "Sorry, I can't see that information; it's in a different computer system. Let me transfer you." Integration exists to create a better experience for me, the customer. Your company just chose not to implement it to save money.

If you are aware that something is hard for a customer and you choose to keep the same process anyway to save costs, that is not empathy—that is greed and a poor brand decision. Adopting an empathetic mindset can and should force your organization to revise policies. Once you see things through the eyes of your customer, you cannot un-see them: changes must be made.

Founder and CEO of Round Table Companies Corey Blake understands this. His firm guides organizations and thought leaders to amplify their purpose in the world through story-telling. Born as a ghostwriting company, the company now works across media, including books, art installations, and documentary films. Blake and his team are often hired to shep-herd authors and storytellers through the book writing and publishing process. For many clients, the stories they're shar-ing are personal and part of their identity. Sharing such stories can make authors feel naked and exposed. Recognizing this, Round Table Companies has changed its processes—and even its core purpose—over the years to better serve its clients.

"When we first began, we were a ghostwriting company, but I had an issue with the lack of authenticity in ghostwrit-ing. That got under my skin," says Blake. "We are still at that boundary. Taking people through this process—which takes a minimum of a year, up to fifteen months for some books—requires a certain amount of vulnerability, which means it requires a certain amount of trust. When we understood what we were asking of our clients, we went back to all of our sys-tems and processes to ask the question, 'Does this enhance or reduce trust?'"

In questioning how every aspect of the process impacted trust, Blake and his team were able to rebuild the company's policies to better align with clients' needs. Clients absolutely have to trust the editors and staff to help them convey ideas and express beliefs fraught with meaning and emotion. "The more a client trusts us, the more willing they are to say things out loud that they have previously been unwilling to say to themselves," Blake says. "And that's where the juicy, gritty, new, evolving stuff lives."

Looking for ways to audit and adapt your customer service policies, processes, and technology to create an empathetic brand experience for your customers? Start here.

- **Provide the big picture.** Properly train employees on the customer's holistic experience and the role they play in that larger journey. It's not about their one little part. Train them on the macro view with the goal of understanding how their piece works within the larger experience. This helps them understand where a customer may be coming from and where they should go next.

- **Empower front-line employees.** Make sure they have all the information they need to make simple judgment calls themselves and solve the majority of customer issues on the spot. This could be financial (offering free returns, discounts, or bonus products) or technological (integrate customer information systems so one person can get a view into whatever the customer requires at that time).

- **Remove all friction for the customer.** Go through every possible process and scenario yourself from the customer's perspective and find the gaps, nuisances, and obstacles that exist. This is user testing, or user-centered design, as discussed earlier. This step is often skipped in the rush to get things up and running. Without this firsthand experience, you will never have empathy. When you find snags, create clear policies to address them.

- **Continually ask for unbiased customer feedback.** Most robo-surveys ask leading questions that cannot be answered in any useful way. They often ask how your experience was with the very last person you spoke to, not capturing the ten people you got transferred to along the frustrating way. Or they ask simply if the problem was solved or not, without any context. If the agent is as helpful as he can possibly be, but company policy ties his hands, then the survey will always show that the problem wasn't solved—and that is not the agent's fault! Or my problem may have been technically "solved" on the phone, but the interaction requires process changes to avoid it happening in the future. The next section devoted to embracing customer feedback dives deeper into this topic.

- **If you ask for customer feedback, *use it*.** Don't make a customer take an experience survey if the results won't lead to policy or process changes. That just wastes everyone's time and energy and will not help the company. And worse: the customer notices.

- **Assume good intent.** Craft policies and processes that show you trust that your customers and employees are ethical and honest people. Yes, some folks will take advantage of lenient policies, but they'll be a very small percentage. Factor that into your costs of doing business or risk alienating everyone else.

5. Accept Feedback as a Gift

The cornerstone of an empathetic brand is listening to your customers. Seems obvious, but how many times have you interacted with organizations that failed to reply to an email, ignored a complaint on Twitter, or refused to acknowledge a bad online review? And if you've had that experience, just imagine how many others have, too.

In 99 percent of cases, people with complaints are not "trolls"; they simply want to be heard. And companies ignore their complaints on both public and private forums at their own peril.

Don't fear feedback of any kind. Use customer feedback, even the most negative stuff, as a catalyst for change. Climb down from the ivory tower and really listen to your customers' experiences to learn what matters through their eyes. For every complaint you get, assume there are hundreds or thousands experiencing that same issue who haven't bothered to contact you. Instead, they just went to your competitor. Think of it this way: every negative review, post, or email complaint is a way to get focus group content for free! And it's far more accurate.

In his bestselling book *Hug Your Haters*, marketing and customer service consultant Jay Baer writes that to truly engage your customers, you must provide multiple methods for collecting customer feedback and responding to customers within the platforms they've used to contact you (rather than driving them to engage with you in another way). For instance, if I send a tweet, I want a customer service response via Twitter, not to be pushed to a website or a phone number. The platform the customer chose is what they prefer. Build your customer service structures to serve your customers across channels. And for the love of Pete, create live interaction mechanisms where possible. If you automate everything, that will simply drive customers crazy and make them hate your brand even more.

Baer cites a great example in a presentation of his BEET (Be Empathetic Every Time) customer service strategy that applies directly to responding to negative feedback. Two casinos received very negative complaints via Facebook. One casino responded with empathy and turned the customer around. The other did not respond at all and not only lost that customer but risked losing all the potential customers who saw the post and witnessed the company's failure to respond. In these parallel circumstances, Baer points out that adding a little bit of empathy can completely change the way the customer perceives the scenario, while simultaneously creating a positive impression for lots of other potential customers watching the interaction unfold in public or through social media. "It's not just one-on-one empathy; it's small group or large group empathy, which is quite a different value proposition, which I find very interesting," he says.

Curvy Yoga founder Anna Guest-Jelley believes an empathetic brand is one that creates a back-and-forth dialogue with its customers. A company that is constantly saying no—or, worse, ignoring complaints because it would rather not deal with conflict—is not serving its clientele. This type of behavior makes the customer feel disrespected when all they want is to be heard.

Of course, this is not about saying "yes" to every request. Again, that is submission, not empathy.

But there should be mechanisms in place for customers to provide feedback, alongside processes that help customer service reps actually do something with that feedback and report back to the customer. You might have the former but not the latter, and that is even more of an issue because now your customers feel ignored.

"If you want your brand to be seen as empathetic and, more importantly, truly *be* empathetic," says Guest-Jelley, "you need to create an environment where it feels like there's a partnership and the company is on the side of their customers and has their best interests at heart."

6. Offer a Personal Touch

Whether your company makes $100,000 or $1 billion in revenue, there are countless opportunities to offer your customers a personal touch. Why should you bother? Because at the end of the day, it is often one person or a handful of people who are interacting directly with your customers. And if those people have the right incentives and support to spend time going the extra mile, your customers will feel understood, valued, and loved.

Alexandra Franzen is a writer and writing teacher who runs retreats, teaches courses, and does private copywriting work for mostly female entrepreneurs. Her clients work across niches and genres from consultants to fitness experts to authors to techies to organic food makers. The primary trait linking her current clients together is a desire to contribute: they, of course, want to make money and sustain their families and livelihoods, but they also want to make the world a better place.

Franzen enjoys consistent sales and books clients up to twelve months in advance, while also filling up her writing workshops. To further prove her success, her email newsletter list is 13,000 strong and growing as of this book's writing, so she has a loyal audience who supports her work and frequently buys from her. (And her email open rates are an unheard-of 30–50 percent, way above the industry average, proving how much her audience engages with her work.) With an average 50,000 to 70,000 website visitors per month, she blogs often and freely shares insights, resources, and tools with her community.

A big part of Franzen's amazing success as a solopreneur is her empathetic philosophy toward her fans and clients. "When I send out an email, I get a lot of responses," she says.

"People write back to share their thoughts and feelings or just say thanks. While it's not always possible, I try, to the best of my ability, to write a personal response to everyone. Even if it's just to say, 'I appreciate you enjoying my work,' I try to treat every single person in my community as a *person*."

The other practice Franzen commits to is to carving out time each week to send some extra love to individual clients. She might simply check in on an important deadline she knows is coming up or reference a challenge they might be facing. One client, for example, was a new mom who was struggling with the adjustment from full-time entrepreneur to full-time entrepreneur and mother. Franzen did not mention any of their current projects but simply reached out to say how proud she was of her and how proud her daughter would be when she was older to see her mom as a strong, creative woman. The woman was so moved that someone was thinking of her. "I do think there's a correlation between sales and empathy," says Franzen. "Every customer at the end of the day wants to know 'You see me and you get me.'"

Franzen's personal touches have carried over into her more expensive writing retreats, where she pens welcome notes, selects custom thank-you gifts for each person to take home with them, and makes sure to spend time one-on-one with each participant. She does these things because she wants to show love and kindness, but they have resulted in almost half of her clients putting down deposits on the next retreat before they've even left the current one.

Franzen runs a small business, which might make it seem easier to offer such personal touches. Many large companies, however, with an empathetic mindset are able to do the same.

Wedgewood Pharmacy is a leading pharmacy in animal health, offering compound medications to veterinarians and pet owners. Founded in 1980, the company has grown from a small local pharmacy to one that now serves more than 50,000 prescribers and hundreds of thousands of patients throughout the U.S. every year. More than twenty years ago, Wedgewood Pharmacy's customer care representatives spontaneously started sending handwritten condolence cards to clients who'd lost their pets. And it made a big impression.

"It began as a conversation," says Daniel Rowan, Wedgewood Pharmacy's vice-president of sales and marketing. "As pet owners ourselves, empathy just leads in every conversation we have about a sick pet. Because we're not typically dealing with a healthy animal. A lot of people don't get a note when their pet dies. But we're dealing with monthly refills, so we sometimes find out faster than even the clients' veterinarian does."

The payoff has been big. Pet owners send notes back, thanking the company for how much it did for their pets. In many cases, Wedgewood Pharmacy's medicines gave the pet and their owner a few more happy years together.

"Hiring empathetic people led to this spontaneous practice that is now something we're known for," says Rowan. "When I travel to trade shows and meet with veterinarians and the caring people who work in their practices, it's not uncommon to have them say, 'Wedgewood, we love you.' They remember us and will talk about how meaningful our cards were to their clients. That helps build loyalty and trust going forward."

And for the pet owners? While many (myself included) might not ever remember the name of their pet's pharmacy, Wedgewood Pharmacy makes a lasting impression. Just check out this prime example of the many emails the company gets, direct from clients:

> Sam went above and beyond typical customer service and I can tell that she loves her job, her smile can be heard

through the phone. Sam was a breath of fresh air during this trying time and I will be letting my vet know how wonderful and professional Wedgewood Pharmacy is.

While this gesture started organically, the company has systematized it so no clients fall through the cracks. This gesture is made a part of new hire training and the rep works with marketing to continue to send off the handwritten notes, not impersonal emails.

As we've seen, such meaningful personal touches can take barely any effort yet mean the world to your customers. CHRISTUS Health's Lisa Reynolds shares that her organization's nurses generally do a bedside report during a shift change, rather than conferring out of sight of the patient like at so many hospitals. They do this intentionally, so the nurses can include the patient in the conversation and have empathy for their concerns. "This gives patients back their dignity, as well as a sense of control, which we understand is so important for them in such a vulnerable time," she says.

Whatever size your organization may be, there is always room to encourage creative thinking and empathy among those working directly with customers. And perhaps even those who do not. Here are some easy-to-implement ideas, but if you do any of them, please resolve to practice these consistently and build rewards or recognition around them so they become a natural part of your customer's experience.

- **Designate "customer love note" days.** Involve everyone in the organization, top to bottom, in sending short, sweet, personalized thank-you notes or emails to select customers. You can even rotate responsibilities each month by department and reward folks for their efforts with a catered lunch or the afternoon off.

- **Implement a customer delight budget.** Your direct account managers or customer service reps could be given discretionary funds for thank-you or personal gifts that show customers you really know them. These could take many shapes, such as coffee shop cards, cookie bouquets, or interesting books. Heck, if you want to be truly memorable and really creative, try gift certificates for arranged deliveries of prepared meals or cleaning or yard services.

- **Encourage quick hits that can be big hits.** Shooting off a brief, unexpected appreciation email or leaving a kind text or voicemail message takes minutes and costs nothing, yet it can have profound ripple effects on customer perception and, yes, bottom-line sales impact.

7. Do Good

Customer loyalty swells when an organization shows empathy for the larger community and world. Philanthropy, when done with genuine intent (not as an empathy veneer!), can transform the brand of an organization from a greedy for-profit engine into a community catalyst and responsible corporate citizen. Such purpose-driven action is key to attracting today's buyers, especially millennials, and to creating brand affinity.

Not only that but doing good and aligning around a larger purpose is a great way to increase employee engagement, which in turn creates a better brand experience for customers. And, as you've read, this unleashes a domino effect: Happy, engaged employees make happier customers. That was Southwest Airlines founder Herb Kelleher's winning philosophy, and research backs up this assertion: companies who master employee engagement improve the customer experience, therefore elevating the brand perception. And round and round we go in a virtuous cycle!

Doing good is often where companies think they have checked the "empathy box," and many choose to stop the conversation there. But as you've read, empathy is more of a mindset than a set of activities; it's an approach that leads to reaching outward to help the larger community and world. Such "do-goodery" cannot live in a vacuum: without the leaders, culture, and policies to support it, philanthropic efforts can be met with a dubious eye. (That darned empathy veneer again.)

TOMS is an example of a company built on empathy that has now turned its giving efforts into an entire brand identity. In 2006, Blake Mycoskie traveled to a small village in Argentina and was moved by seeing children with no shoes on their feet. He intentionally founded TOMS to help and vowed that for every pair of shoes it sold, the company would donate a pair to a child in need. The idea took off as the One for One® model and expanded into its subsequent brands: TOMS Eyewear promises that with every pair of glasses purchased, TOMS helps restore sight to a person in need; TOMS Roasting Co. Coffee provides one week of clean water to a person in need when you buy a bag of coffee. As Mycoskie puts it, "We didn't start a company with a mission, but we had a mission that turned into a company."

TOMS' success includes growing the company and expanding their giving efforts. According to the company's website, as of this writing, it has given away more than 35 million pairs of shoes and helped restore sight to more than 250,000 people. This approach has been so successful for the brand that many other companies—including online sock retailer Bombas, eyeglass company Warby Parker, and toiletry vendor Soapbox—have adopted a similar one-for-one model. United by Blue, a sustainable outdoor goods and apparel company, takes this even further: according to its website, for every product sold, it removes one pound of trash from the world's oceans and waterways.

Mycoskie believes all this giving, while a cost, creates competitive advantage. "Built into our cost structure is the intention to provide great benefit to our customers because they feel like they're getting to be part of something more than just a transaction," he explains. "More and more understand the impact of their purchases on the rest of the world. By doing that, we're able to gain more loyal customers; we're attracting new customers. While we spend a ton of money on giving, we also feel that there's a real return on that investment."

Any sized organization, even a one-person shop, can put empathy into action by doing good. Writing teacher Alexandra Franzen infuses empathy into her business—and encourages her clients to as well—by incorporating charitable actions into her for-profit business. She sets aside revenue every month to support charities she believes in. For one of her online classes, she donated a portion of every tuition payment to the American Civil Liberties Union. "I've just built that into the budget for the class," she says. "We state that on the website and it gets people excited to know their money is also going to help others."

At Reed Tech, Dave Ballai says the company is willing to absorb some costs if doing so enables employees to give back to the community. "Every employee is entitled to at least two full service days a year to do anything they choose, and the interesting thing is a lot of them go on their own time to stay dedicated to these organizations," he says. "It's great to see. This not only sounds good to external customers: it's also a way to further create an internal culture of empathy."

Many successful companies have built "doing good" into their bones. Technology giant Salesforce has always held a dual focus: being a leader in the customer relationship management space but also in larger society. Marc Benioff—its founder, chairman, and CEO—is quoted as saying, "Companies can do more than just make money, they can serve others. The business of business is improving the state of the world."

The company is proud of its 1-1-1 model, which aims to use its technology, people, and resources to improve communities all over the world. This model of donating 1 percent of product, employee time, and resources became Salesforce.org, the non-profit social enterprise of Salesforce. Since 1999, the company has donated more than $260 million in grants to the community, 40,000 non-profits and higher education institutions use the technology for free or at a steep discount, and Salesforce employees have donated 3.6 million hours of volunteer time.

This emphasis on doing good has paid off: the company exceeds $13 billion in annual revenue, has consistently landed on the *Forbes* Most Innovative Companies list, and enjoys benefits such as high employee engagement and retention. And this ripple effect of impact not only builds Salesforce's brand reputation, it also gives employees a sense of purpose and pride, which shows up in their work and their roles as company brand ambassadors.

Unilever experienced similar revenue and engagement benefits when it launched its Sustainable Living Plan in 2009 to help increase their positive social impact while reducing their environmental footprint. Since the initiative launched, the company claims that its sustainable brands have grown 46 percent faster than the rest of the business and delivered 70 percent of its turnover growth. It also claims that it is on track to meet 80 percent of its ambitious plan goals, "which include improving health and wellbeing for one billion people, reducing environmental impact by half, and enhancing livelihoods for its millions of employees, suppliers, and retailers."

Beyond that, a 2017 *Forbes* article stated that since Unilever shifted course to focus on purpose and profits, it "witnessed its market capitalization rise from €63 billion to over €100 billion while its earnings per share grew from 1.16 to almost 2.00."

Philanthropy, giving back, doing good—it can take almost infinite forms, so I won't compile specific action items for you here. In fact, setting your leadership team to the task of exploring the most brand-aligned ways that your company can support its community is a fantastic path to embed empathy organically.

The more your efforts relate to your mission, the more authentic and believable it is, and it gives your employees an even deeper sense of loyalty and purpose. If you sell pet food and supplies, it's natural your organization might support local pet shelters or take a stand against pet abuse. If you develop HR and recruiting software, giving back to local job training programs or providing career mentoring to college students makes perfect sense. Get the team together to revisit your mission and purpose, and you may find natural philanthropic efforts to support.

8. Ask . . . and Echo Back

Empathy is all about getting out of your own head. And so is building a great brand.

One of the most important brand strategies I share with my clients is to talk with their ideal clients or customers on a regular basis. This is the only way to stay connected to what those people are thinking, feeling, or craving. If your brand is really empathetic, it will know its customers so well that it makes those customers feel like the organization is reading their minds.

We're not talking about using tracking software or user analytics, although both provide great ways to see things from the customer's point of view. We're talking about good old-fashioned engagement. If individuals and leaders practice the art of listening—as was discussed in the section about empathetic leadership traits—this next step will be an easy one. Simply listening to and hearing your customers' struggles, fears, insecurities, and challenges and then echoing those back in their language will result in deeper brand loyalty, higher sales conversion, and more referrals. When you offer to solve a problem your customers have and express your solution in a way that resonates with them, they cannot help but feel that your solution is tailor-made for them.

While outright asking your customers about the challenges they face or the benefits they seek through qualitative interviews or surveys can help you land on their exact words, some experts suggest mining unconventional sources, such as Amazon reviews. This is how one famous conversion copywriter, Joanna Wiebe, came up with the perfect website home page headline for one of her clients: "If you think you need rehab, you do." That headline generated a 400 percent increase in button clicks for Beachway, a rehab and addiction therapy center. It crushed the control headline, "Your Addiction Ends Here," so incredibly that it led to a 20 percent increase in form submits—even though the form was on an entirely separate page.

Method cleaning products have some of the most entertaining and witty messages written on their packaging, like on the back of its Antibac All-Purpose Cleaner: "You think you're so smart, don't you? Well... you are, okay? You win." When writing product descriptions and instructions, the company makes even complicated but required technical and safety information easy to understand—keeping it real for those who have to use such products when cleaning up unpleasant messes or doing laundry. The website products page headline is just one example of copy that sounds like its customers talk: *Shop Method for products that clean like heck + smell like heaven.* The company's marketing voice directly connects to the voices inside its customers' heads. Or at least the voice in my head, and I'm a loyal customer, often driving out of my way to buy Method products.

Copywriter Joel Klettke amusingly gives some modified examples to better speak your customers' language in a 2017 Unbounce talk, "How to Read Your Customers' Minds." He cites the difference between company headlines written to say what the marketing team wants to say, not what customers want to hear, such as, "Sales made simple" versus "You hate guesswork and busywork so we made sales less work." Or "Break through native reporting limitations" versus "Get the reports your CRM can't give you—without the headache it does."

This is a much more empathetic approach to marketing than diluting your message with jargon, corporate-speak, and blather that *you* deem important. Many companies make the branding mistake of falling in love with their own articulation of problems and solutions, when they'd be better served asking their customers how *they* describe the challenges they face.

I often tell my clients to imagine their ideal customer in situ. What are they saying to themselves or complaining to their spouse about or muttering in frustration under their breath? I'm willing to bet they are not grumbling over happy-hour margaritas using phrases like, "You know, I really need a best-in-class solution" or "I struggle to maximize productivity while increasing profits." Customer are probably saying things like, "I need to process claims faster" or "How do I lead my team to be more efficient and work together better so we can move faster?"

Articulate the problem you solve in *their* language, not yours. If your brand supports it, you can even use some of the more... ahem, *colorful* language they may use in real life to express their pain. Nothing will get a prospect's head nodding in agreement faster than seeing themselves in the picture you are painting.

In many cases, you and your employees may have no concept of what your customers' lives are like, no matter how much you think you know about the market. This is when you really need to dig in, act with empathy, and ask questions.

Candace Nicolls is senior vice-president of Snagger Services at Snag, a marketplace that connects hourly workers and employers. The company identifies so strongly with their brand that they call themselves Snaggers (hence her title), but really Nicolls runs human resources and recruiting. Most Snaggers are highly skilled software engineers, many of whom have no concept of what it's like to support a family as an hourly worker. But they must identify with their customers in order to serve them.

"The cycle of poverty is so frustrating because it's so hard to get out of it. The things that you and I might consider to be a nuisance are a complete setback for the people that we're here to serve every day," says Nicolls. "Most of our internal people are not facing the same problems our workers are facing, so we constantly remind them that we're not solving for what we think are their problems, we need to solve what they're actually struggling with."

How can you ask and echo back within your own organization? Here are some ways to uncover your customers' needs, prove that you hear them, and ensure your solutions are exactly the right ones.

- **Create an open-question survey.** Use this tool to gather feedback and give an incentive for customer participation. These can be fancy ones done by expensive research firms or easy ones you create yourself using SurveyMonkey for free or perhaps a short Google form. The open questions encourage customers to use the words they would naturally choose to articulate the issues, so you can echo back.

- **Ask customers a thought-provoking question via email and invite them to hit reply.** This is a great way to get more out of your automated email responses. If you offer a welcome email or an order confirmation, use that as opportunity to gather intelligence. About a month or so ago, I asked my email list which adjective they'd use to describe the "brand" they'd like to have. The results were enlightening. This technique has helped me write better marketing materials that instantly resonate with the right people.

- **Interview them individually by phone or take select customers out for coffee.** Such intimate interactions can also serve to build stronger relationships while helping you glean important insights. Make time to take individual customers or prospects out to lunch or coffee and don't sell: just listen. Ask them what they are struggling with, what are their biggest challenges, what solutions they have tried. Make note of the exact words and phrases they use. In the past, I have reached out to a few beloved clients or colleagues who match my ideal client persona to ask them what they want and need as it relates to my services. The feedback was amazing and has helped me shape my courses and other offerings.

- **Host an event focused on customer desires.** No need for stuffy (and expensive) focus groups. Gather a group of them together and encourage them to share their needs, desires, goals, and fears in a safe environment. Document the exact words they use (so you can ask and echo back!). Perhaps a wine and cheese reception would be fun, or an informal panel discussion with a question and answer session afterward.

- **Scout social media and online reviews.** Quick and dirty. Review what people are saying of their own accord without prompting about your industry, products, or services. How do they express their frustration? What features do they often praise? What do they say the product or service enables them to do? Make note of the words and phrases being used and weave that into your messaging.

Mike Michalowicz—marketing consultant, speaker, and author of such bestsellers as *The Toilet Paper Entrepreneur* and *Profit First*—advises you to collect customer information face to face whenever possible. "You've got to see them in their own environment, otherwise they won't trust you," he explains. "Help them be comfortable so they will speak from the heart. You've got to see the makeup of people. You've got to live with your customer."

Not only does he attend live conferences to constantly connect with his customers, but he has literally moved in with them! "I've rented a cabin in Denver and invited my top consulting clients for retreats," says Michalowicz. "For four days, we cook, play cards, talk shop. This helps me understand my customers as family and get inside their minds."

Follow his example by reaching out to your existing customers, prospects, or colleagues who fit your ideal customer profile. Send them a quick note, prepare a few direct and simple questions to discuss, and be respectful of their time. And always offer a thank-you for their feedback: a discount, free guide, gift card, chocolate basket, or donation to a charity they love.

Your brand perception relies on how you conduct business every day. Whether your audience is customers, clients, donors, or partners, if you're not attuned to what they want and need, your brand will never be seen as empathetic. The foundations of this external brand rely on internal authenticity: the right people creating the right culture, striving day in and day out to deliver a connective customer experience. Building a brand that inspires lifelong loyalty starts by determining what the audience needs and creating connections—from user-centric product design to delightful customer experiences that might add up to making your community (and the world) a better place.

> You can download an empathetic brand practices reference sheet at www.the empathyedge.com/ resources to start implementing these ideas and delighting your customers.

Sharpen Your Empathy Edge

Here are eight strategies to help you engage, connect with, and delight your customers on a regular basis, all while serving something more significant than your bottom line.

1 **Align on mission:** Your mission should not simply be a trite platitude. It needs to be crafted in such a way that it informs every action that employees take on a daily basis. It's equally important to make sure your mission aligns with your customer's values. To build a truly empathetic brand, you must respect how your customers see the world.

2 **Speak your customer's language:** Choosing the right words is the start of the empathetic brand conversation. Think about the most important and resonant words for your audience. Which words will make them feel alienated or condescended to? Which will make them feel valued, heard, and understood? What is the voice inside their heads saying?

3 **Hire people who are passionate about customers:** While it's true that every employee should embrace and reflect empathy, the brand lives in the actions of the people who represent the company and help end-consumers get what they need. Your people are your most important brand assets, and that means hiring the right brand ambassadors, people who can take the right actions and deliver the promised, expected experience.

4 **Implement the right customer service policies:** Today's technology and emphasis on transparency mean front-line employees are now closer to the customer than ever before. It also means these same employees should have the authority to address problems on the spot, based on each unique circumstance.

5 **Accept feedback as a gift:** Don't fear feedback of any kind. Use customer feedback, even the most negative stuff, as a catalyst for change.

6 **Offer a personal touch:** Whether your company makes $100,000 or $1 billion, there are countless opportunities to offer your customers a personal touch and make them feel understood and valued.

7 **Do good:** Customer loyalty swells when an organization shows empathy for the larger community and world. Such purpose-driven action (when done genuinely) is key to attracting today's buyers, especially millennials, and to creating brand affinity.

8 Ask... and echo back: Simply listening to and hearing your customers' struggles, fears, insecurities, and challenges and then echoing those back in their language will result in deeper brand loyalty, higher sales conversion, and more referrals.

CONCLUSION
More Empathy, More Success

Empathy has no script. There is no right way or wrong way to do it. It's simply listening, holding space, withholding judgment, emotionally connecting, and communicating that incredibly healing message of "You're not alone."
BRENÉ BROWN

NJECTING MORE EMPATHY into your leadership style, company culture, and brand actions may seem like relatively insignificant steps, especially when you scroll through the daily news headlines and see war, famine, cruelty, and ignorance writ large. But making the world a more compassionate place is a task that must be attacked from multiple fronts. Fortunately, you can dedicate yourself to working within your own sphere of influence and trust that empathy building is also happening much earlier in the learning curve.

In case you missed it, this book has a larger, sneakier mission: not just to help leaders like you and brands like yours succeed by adopting an empathy mindset but to ultimately create a more empathetic world. We're just starting in a very specific context: work.

So, take heart.

Fostering the Next Generation of Empathetic Leaders

There are efforts afoot all over the world to foster the next generation of empathetic leaders. Inspirational visionaries are working to help make empathy such an embedded part of the way people operate that we won't even need to have to think about it—or perhaps, one day, even write books about it. After all, do we write books about how to blink or make our hearts beat?

From a beautiful and calming campus in El Cerrito, California, just outside of San Francisco, Yalda Modabber and her team of teachers are shaping the next generation of mindful and empathetic changemakers. Modabber is the executive director of Golestan Kids, a non-profit organization that uses its innovative pre-K to fifth grade school as a model for educators worldwide. Here, empathy and kindness are integrated into every aspect of the curriculum and environment. While other schools make noble attempts to inject empathy into their programming, Golestan prioritizes it as the core of each child's experience.

"Kids here feel respected and cared for," says Modabber. And she should know. As a little girl, she experienced what happens when children don't get enough empathy and kindness. Born in Boston, her family moved back to Tehran, Iran, when she was a child. In 1979, the Iranian Revolution brought her family back to Boston; that same year, sixty Americans were taken hostage at the U.S. Embassy in Iran. It was not a great time to be an Iranian living in the States.

Modabber felt isolated as an Iranian immigrant and didn't have any friends. One day, some kids knocked on her door, asking if she could come out and play; she was delighted and her mother was ecstatic. When the girls took her around the corner, she found a mob of kids who taunted her and pelted her with plastic bags filled with plaster. Modabber was emotionally and physically bullied for another two years after that. These experiences inspired her to create Golestan, an organization that exists to ensure that none of her students ever grow up to treat others so heartlessly.

Modabber is a scientist by training and has a keen understanding of the way the brain works, which fuels her work with children. "There's a lot of talk about empathy, but I personally use the word 'kindness' a lot, as I believe it's integral," she says. "For me personally, I think that goes back to my experience as a child. It's important for me that my children be kind, and in order to be kind, I believe they need to be empathetic. And in order to be empathetic, you need to be able to see and feel other people's perspectives."

Surrounding the kids with beauty is a key element of the school's philosophy. Flowers are placed on the tables and all over the school, often picked from the school's edible garden. The teachers are trained not to over-clutter the walls and spaces so that the classrooms are calming and beautiful. They are exposed to different cultures through immersion in foreign languages, curricula, materials, and even the food they eat—and they take time to be grateful for where their food comes from and for those hands that prepared it.

Research has proven that humans are born with an innate sense of empathy, but that does not let us off the hook from tending to it and encouraging it to grow. "Actually, I think the biggest factor is learning," says Modabber. "I think someone who's not predisposed to be sensitive to other people's needs can absolutely learn this, and someone who is predisposed to be sensitive to other people's needs, if it's not nurtured in them, can lose it entirely."

Goelstan's goal is to provide children with "native fluency" in empathy, so that it becomes intuitive and they don't even have to think about it. Being kind and empathetic becomes their identity, their default setting when interacting with others. When they self-identify as "a kind person," anything they do which goes against that identity creates cognitive dissonance. They think, *This isn't who I am*, and course-correct automatically.

This is the beauty of nurturing empathy at a young age. It's embedded in everything one says and does and doesn't have to be "learned." But although early adoption has its advantages, that doesn't mean it's too late for adults to cultivate empathy within themselves.

"Yes, empathy needs to be nurtured in children but once you become an adult, it becomes a choice. It's a different type of empathy that's more proactive," Modabber says. "If an adult wants to perceive themselves as a 'kind person,' if this is who they want to be, they need to make intentional choices to support this identity. It requires ongoing work, but I believe one can indeed nurture empathy and kindness in oneself and in other people."

With this in mind, many of us choose to cultivate empathy in our households, our families, our communities, and our personal lives. But as this book has shown, the logical next step is to encourage empathetic mindsets and compassionate action in our careers and workplaces. To spread empathy further and faster, we must use our influence as leaders and employees, mentors and managers to foster business environments that are supportive, customer-centric, and flexible. Doing so can only benefit our companies and our world. But it might not feel like a walk in the park.

I won't sugarcoat it: this work can be hard.

Whether you are trying to cultivate empathy for yourself, your team, or your customers, it takes courage to admit something is lacking and go out of your comfort zone to change the game. You need bravery to combat personal feelings of jealousy, fear, and intimidation. We all come to this work with our own baggage—that includes your company culture or brand.

"This is going to be hard. It's going to be uncomfortable, but it's okay to find it difficult," says psychologist Susan Spinrad Esterly. "It's okay to have to dig deep and have faith. There's nothing to lose and everything to gain."

How much you gain is not guaranteed. But hopefully this book has given you ample proof that there are huge personal and organizational benefits to adopting an empathetic mindset in the business context and acting with compassion—enough proof that you will at least *try*. By implementing a few key tactics from this book, you will increase the odds of having a good outcome or at least a different outcome. Remember:

- Empathy spurs innovation—as shifts at Microsoft and research at Google proved.
- Empathy aligns you to customer wants and needs—as the success of Apple, REI, JetBlue, Snag, and Airbnb exemplify.
- Empathy improves employee performance and engagement—as the cultures of Next Jump and Kronos demonstrate, and as research from Gallup, Businessolver, and Google shows.
- Empathetic leaders cultivate loyalty and a better working environment—as Reed Tech's Dave Ballai, Microsoft's Satya Nadella, CHRISTUS Health's Lisa Reynolds, and multiple studies have shown.
- Empathy drives growth, sales, and financial success—as results from Brighton Jones, Salesforce, TOMS, and Chobani prove to the market.

You and your organization may have gotten very far over the years doing things the way they've always been done. And you may have picked up this book with a sense of skepticism. But you wouldn't have read it if you didn't have some sense that things could be different, better, or more successful—whether for you as an individual or for your entire organization.

Keep the faith. Have the courage to try to operate differently. Increase your odds of producing a positive result, or at least creating an environment for yourself that breeds understanding and compassion. And be bold enough to lead the rallying cry, even if your voice is the only one at first.

It Starts with You

Ashoka is the world's largest network of social entrepreneurs. The organization pioneered the field thirty-five years ago and has since supported more than 3,500 Ashoka Fellows across the globe, guiding them to grow unexpected ideas into transformative social progress. The organization further expanded its global impact with the Empathy Initiative. Launched together with leading social entrepreneurs and pioneer educators, the movement seeks to embed empathy and changemaking more deeply into the U.S. education landscape. You've heard from several Ashoka Fellows in this book, including Eric Dawson of Peace First, Dina Buchbinder of Educación para Compartir, and Joy McBrien of Fair Anita.

Michael Zakaras, Ashoka's U.S. director for strategy and partnerships, told me about how most Ashoka Fellows had experiences early on in their lives that impacted how they see the world and formed their commitment to making a difference. They became focused on finding the solution, rather than complaining about the problem. And they put empathy into action. Zakaras asks, "If we learn that it's important for changemakers to start on that path early in life, then isn't it our responsibility to give more kids those kinds of experiences? That means emphasizing empathy but also creating opportunities for young people to act on it and feel powerful. It means new educational and parenting priorities, new ways of hiring, and more. It's a major shift but a necessary one if we want a world of changemakers working for the good of all."

Become the type of leader and company that emphasizes solutions and that helps others—employees, customers—get on the path early. Build empathy into the very foundation of your company, and watch the ripple effects.

Concerned that you'll be championing these changes entirely on your own? Remember that creating a more empathetic workplace culture, brand, and ultimately world can start with just one person sparking change.

No matter what your organization is like now, anyone at any level can make change by acting with more empathy within their own sphere of influence. Keep the faith, because the changes won't happen overnight.

"The more you can come at this from a place of curiosity, seeking to understand, the more likely you'll be able to make change and move your career and business forward," says The Innovare Group CEO Kim Bohr. "Because you'll see opportunities that you might not have seen if you weren't looking at this from a place of empathy."

Bohr's consultancy helps funded startups and midsized growth organizations boost performance, so they can compete more effectively, lead the market, and create a legacy. She works with companies from the inside out to solve problems, and often she sees that what seem to be operational issues— missed product development dates, market share loss, or cost overruns—can actually be attributed to poor internal communication and the inability to recognize diverse perspectives. And at their core? People who play the blame game and refuse to see others' points of view.

Because of the fast pace of business today, Bohr has witnessed a counterproductive tendency to try to change others first, whether that looks like executives faulting workers or the rank-and-file giving up because they believe management will never change. The reality is that waiting for others to make the needed changes we want to see stalls our own causes, careers, and goals.

"A more successful approach, regardless of your level or role," says Bohr, "is to take responsibility for your own actions and behaviors. What is within your control? Instead of saying, 'If *they* were different, things would be better,' we should ask ourselves, 'What step can *I* take now that will move me forward and give me the outcome I seek?'"

Start with yourself. Model curiosity, make small changes, encourage others, listen. Then find ways to let your actions create ripple effects throughout your group, department, division, and company. Because it may start with you, but the goal is for your empathetic shifts to reach well *beyond* you.

Empathy Is Everything

I love the idea of starting small while thinking big— remembering that all journeys begin with a single step but also actively envisioning those journeys as bold, daring, far-reaching, and life-altering. I think that building a more empathetic world can follow that same model. We begin with ourselves, our spheres, our companies, but keep in mind that we're becoming role models for the next generation. Seeing us strive to make empathy a part of everything—from education to government, industry to science, institutions to individuals—will encourage young people to do the same.

It may feel like a lot of responsibility, and it is. But empathy is all about thinking beyond our own experiences, feeling outward from ourselves, and envisioning a shared future. If we just work on ourselves, our teams, and our organizations, we're missing the point entirely. Catalyzing empathy in our workplaces gives us a huge advantage over our less compassionate competitors, but the real endgame is to make the whole world more open, curious, and understanding. The true goal is to make our offices and corporate campuses the empathetic proving grounds that spark change across the globe.

We're ready, and the world is waiting. So let's knuckle down and get to it.

ACKNOWLEDGMENTS

THERE'S OFTEN ONLY room for one author on the cover, but honestly this book would not have been possible without many people. It takes a village, as they say!

Big thank-you to Greg Nelson, a gifted strengths coach, for first guiding me to this empathy-writing path. To Alexandra Franzen for helping me first coalesce the idea and articulate the book, as your words propelled me forward.

Thank you to Jesse, Amanda, Rony, Peter, Annemarie, Crissy, and the entire team at Page Two Strategies for believing in me and in this topic. You are all amazing storytelling shepherds.

Authors often say this, but this time it's ridiculously true. This book would *not* have been written without the incomparable Sally McGraw's unwavering support. Your writing, editing, coaching, and tough love drove me to keep going and get this book into the world. I'm eternally grateful to know you.

Thank you to all the wonderful leaders, marketers, and experts who shared their stories and insights for the book: Jay Baer, Dave Ballai, Parissa Behnia, Corey Blake, Kimberly Bohr, Dina Buchbinder, Cory Custer, Eric Dawson, Erica Dhawan, Stacey Engle, Susan Spinrad Esterly, Alexandra Franzen, Christina Harbridge, Sally Hogshead, Anna Guest-Jelley, Zanette Johnson, Jon Jones, Ellen Petry Leanse, Josh Levine, Andrew Marks, Joy McBrien, Lisa Earle McLeod,

Renee Metty, Yalda Modabber, Candace Nicolls, Belinda Parmar, Linda J. Popky, Lisa Reynolds, Rebecca Friese Rodskog, Dan Rowan, Rae Shanahan (and Kristin Korzan for your help!), and Ben Steele. And a big thank-you to those who generously gave me their time for interviews but for various reasons we were not able to include their valuable content.

Thank you to Gina Baleria, Melody Biringer, Dia Bondi, Amanda Canning, Samantha DenBleyker, Kristi Dosh, Kimberly Harris, Brigette Iarusso, Whitney Keyes, Elsa Kitts, Tracy Klinkroth, Kristin Lamoreaux, Michelle Tillis Lederman, Rebecca Friese Rodskog, Lisen Stromberg, and Mary Trigiani for your generous input, connections, and support along the way. And special thank you, Kristin, for inviting me to speak and test-drive this topic at the SIM Women Conference early on. The enthusiastic response from those leaders kept me going.

Thank you to the fierce, generous, eloquent women of the Authoress group. It's such a thrill to be part of this family. You are all proof that when women help other women, it creates exponential impact. Special thanks to Denise Brousseau, Melinda Byerley, Dorie Clark, Erica Dhawan, Ange Friesen, Sarah Granger, Michelle Tillis Lederman, Marti Konstant, Elisa Camahort Page, Linda J. Popky, and Michele Wucker for your generous connections, support, and input. #StrongerTogether

Thank you to my family for your support and love. And to my mom, smiling down from Heaven, who always encouraged me to write.

Thank you to my husband, Paul, for his constant faith and his ability to often get dinner on the table or pick up our son from school while I typed away. Your partnership and love make every dream possible.

To all the organizations big and small who are trying to make the world a better place by leading with empathy, rock on! No matter how big your sphere of influence, do work you're proud of and treat your teams and customers with compassion. Change the game about what business success means. The world needs your bravery now more than ever.

Most importantly, this book is for my beautiful boy, Callum. Seeing the world through a preschooler's eyes has been my empathy practice of late, and it's glorious. Dear one, it is for you and your generation that I'm doing what I can to persuade people that empathy is the ultimate winning strategy in business and life. My hope, my love, is that this book, like many others of this genre, helps transform people and creates a world for you that is worthy of your kindness, curiosity, and unconditional love. Always know you can be competitive *and* kind. Innovative *and* compassionate. You can lead effectively *and* be respectful of those who disagree with you. Don't let anyone ever tell you otherwise. You are not the only person in this world: always be open to seeing things through others' perspectives so that you can lead and act with compassion, no matter what you choose you do in this life.

FURTHER READING

TO FUEL YOUR own interest on empathy, please enjoy these wonderful books that tackle the topic from diverse perspectives. Many were referenced throughout this work, but some are additional recommendations that can richly enhance your empathy exploration.

WorkInspired: How to Build an Organization Where Everyone Loves to Work by Aron Ain (McGraw-Hill Education, 2018)

Hug Your Haters: How to Embrace Complaints and Keep Your Customers by Jay Baer (Portfolio, 2016)

Talk Triggers: The Complete Guide to Creating Customers with Word of Mouth by Jay Baer and Daniel Lemin (Portfolio, 2018)

Against Empathy: The Case for Rational Compassion by Paul Bloom (Ecco, 2016)

Dare to Lead: Brave Work. Tough Conversations. Whole Hearts. by Brené Brown (Random House, 2018)

Better Allies: Everyday Actions to Create Inclusive, Engaging Workplaces by Karen Catlin (Better Allies Press, 2019)

When Things Fall Apart: Heart Advice for Difficult Times by Pema Chödrön (Shambhala Classics, anniversary edition, 2016)

Get Big Things Done: The Power of Connectional Intelligence by Erica Dhawan and Saj-nicole Joni (St. Martin's Press, 2015)

Emotional Intelligence: Why It Can Matter More Than IQ by Daniel Goleman (Bantam, 2006)

Empathy by Daniel Goleman, Annie McKee, and Adam Waytz (Harvard Business Review Press, 2017)

The Power of Moments: Why Certain Experiences Have Extraordinary Impact by Chip Heath and Dan Heath (Simon & Schuster, 2017)

Fascinate: How to Make Your Brand Impossible to Resist by Sally Hogshead (HarperBusiness, 2016)

Amaze Every Customer Every Time: 52 Tools for Delivering the Most Amazing Customer Service on the Planet by Shep Hyken (Greenleaf Book Group Press, 2013)

An Everyone Culture: Becoming a Deliberately Developmental Organization by Robert Kegan, Lisa Laskow Lahey, Matthew L. Miller, and Andy Fleming (Harvard Business Review Press, 2016)

Empathy: Why It Matters, and How to Get It by Roman Krznaric (TarcherPerigee, 2014)

The Connector's Advantage: 7 Mindsets to Grow Your Influence and Impact by Michelle Tillis Lederman (Page Two, 2019)

The 11 Laws of Likability: Relationship Networking... Because People Do Business with People They Like by Michelle Tillis Lederman (AMACOM, 2011)

The Pivot: Orchestrating Extraordinary Business Momentum by Lori Michele Leavitt (Abridge Media, 2017)

Great Mondays: How to Design a Company Culture Employees Love by Josh Levine (McGraw-Hill Education, 2018)

Magnificent Leadership: Transform Uncertainty, Transcend Circumstance, Claim the Future by Sarah Levitt (Business Expert Press, 2017)

Leading with Noble Purpose: How to Create a Tribe of True Believers by Lisa Earle McLeod (Wiley, 2016)

Selling with Noble Purpose: How to Drive Revenue and Do Work That Makes You Proud by Lisa Earle McLeod (Wiley, 2012)

The Triangle of Truth: The Surprisingly Simple Secret to Solving Conflicts Large and Small by Lisa Earle McLeod (Tarcher-Perigee, 2011)

Breaking Through "Bitch": How Women Can Shatter Stereotypes and Lead Fearlessly by Carol Vallone Mitchell (Career Press, 2015)

Hit Refresh: The Quest to Rediscover Microsoft's Soul and Imagine a Better Future for Everyone by Satya Nadella, Greg Shaw, and Jill Tracie Nichols (HarperBusiness, 2017)

Pause: Harnessing the Life-Changing Power of Giving Yourself a Break by Rachael O'Meara (TarcherPerigee, 2017)

Drive: The Surprising Truth about What Motivates Us by Daniel H. Pink (Riverhead Books, 2009)

Marketing above the Noise: Achieve Strategic Advantage with Marketing That Matters by Linda J. Popky (Routledge, 2015)

Ignite Your Sales Power!: Mindfulness Skills for Sales Professionals by Joy Rains (Whole Earth Press, 2017)

Branding Basics for Small Business: How to Create an Irresistible Brand on Any Budget by Maria Ross (NorLights Press, 2nd Edition, 2014)

Pour Your Heart Into It: How Starbucks Built a Company One Cup at a Time by Howard Schultz (Hyperion, 1997)

How We Work: Live Your Purpose, Reclaim Your Sanity, and Embrace the Daily Grind by Leah Weiss, PhD (Harper Wave, 2018)

NOTES

Introduction

"PFCC is a global movement..." Institute for Patient and Family
    Centered Care, ipfcc.org.

"core pillars of PFCC..." Institute for Patient and Family Centered Care,
    ipfcc.org/about/pfcc.html.

"These hospitals are seeing..." Aaron M. Clay and Bridget Parsh,
    "Patient- and Family-Centered Care," *AMA Journal of Ethics* (January
    2016), journalofethics.ama-assn.org/article/patient-and-family-
    centered-care-its-not-just-pediatrics-anymore/2016-01.

"economist Milton Friedman's view..." Angel Gonzalez, "Starbucks as
    Citizen," *Seattle Times* (March 15, 2015), seattletimes.com/business/
    starbucks/starbucks-as-citizen-schultz-goes-bold.

"Schultz said, 'The size and the scale...'" Ibid.

"Advertiser 84 Lumber chose to..." Bethonie Butler and Maura
    Judkis, "The Five Most Political Super Bowl Commercials," *The
    Washington Post* (February 6, 2017), washingtonpost.com/news/
    arts-and-entertainment/wp/2017/02/06/the-five-most-political-
    super-bowl-commercials/?utm_term=.020ad91cfa4a.

"Audi presented a charming story..." Ibid.

"The average American, for example,..." Marguerite Ward, "A Brief
    History of the 8-Hour Workday, Which Changed How Americans
    Work," CNBC.com (May 3, 2017), cnbc.com/2017/05/03/how-the-
    8-hour-workday-changed-how-americans-work.html.

"tech futurist Christina 'CK' Kerley..." Email with author, September 11,
    2018.

Chapter 1: Empathy Explored

"Christina Harbridge was an eighteen-year-old college student..."
Interview with author, September 5, 2017.

"as opposed to the typical 9.9 percent..." A number provided by ACA
(American Collectors Association) in the 1990s. This story and data
are from twenty years ago. According to the ACA's 2010 industry
benchmarking report, these rates fluctuate each year and it has
changed how the rate is calculated, but the 2010 median liquidation
percentage (or debt recovery rate) was still cited as 11.7 percent
in its most recent report (acainternational.org/assets/industry-
research-statistics/2010-benchmarking-survey.pdf).

"The word *sympathy*, which stems..." "Sympathy (n.)," *Online Etymology
Dictionary*, etymonline.com/word/sympathy?ref=etymonline_
crossreference.

"'it tends to convey commiseration..." "Empathy vs. Sympathy,"
Dictionary.com, dictionary.com/e/empathy-vs-sympathy.

"*Empathy*, introduced centuries later..." "Empathy vs. Sympathy,"
Dictionary.com, dictionary.com/e/empathy-vs-sympathy.

"Parissa Behnia, executive coach, business consultant..." Interview with
author, January 30, 2018.

"Sara Schairer, founder and CEO of Compassion It..." Sara Schairer,
"What's the Difference between Empathy, Sympathy, and
Compassion?" The Chopra Center, chopra.com/articles/
whats-the-difference-between-empathy-sympathy-and-compassion.

"former military personnel homelessness..." Leo Shane III, "Number of
Homeless Vets Rises for First Time in Seven Years," *Military Times*
(December 6, 2017), militarytimes.com/veterans/2017/12/06/
number-of-homeless-veterans-nationwide-rises-for-first-time-in-
seven-years/.

"Psychologist Paul Bloom..." Paul Bloom, *Against Empathy: The Case for
Rational Compassion* (Ecco, 2016).

"To illustrate, he cites a study..." Ibid.

"Bloom states, 'Empathy is like..." Ibid.

"concept of survival of the fittest..." Fun fact: Darwin did not coin the
phrase "survival of the fittest." It was philosopher Herbert Spencer.

"our modern definition of *empathy*..." Roman Krznaric, *Empathy: Why It
Matters, and How to Get It* (TarcherPerigee, 2014).

"according to Krznaric..." Ibid.

"Barack Obama urged graduates..." Barack Obama, "Xavier University
Commencement Address" (2006), obamaspeeches.com/087-Xavier-
University-Commencement-Address-Obama-Speech.htm.

"Author and leadership expert Simon Sinek..." Shelley Levitt, "Why the Empathetic Leader Is the Best Leader," *Success* (March 15, 2017), success.com/article/why-the-empathetic-leader-is-the-best-leader.

"First, social psychology distinguishes..." Lesley University, "The Psychology of Emotional and Cognitive Empathy," lesley.edu/ article/the-psychology-of-emotional-and-cognitive-empathy.

"But *cognitive empathy* means..." "Cognitive vs. Emotional Empathy with Daniel Goleman," Key Step Media, video, keystepmedia.com/ cognitive-emotional-empathy/#.WT7gbRPyvOQ.

"A 2017 Forbes.com article states..." Billee Howard, "Top 3 Disruptive Marketing Trends for 2018," Forbes.com, forbes.com/sites/ billeehoward/2017/11/12/disruptive-marketing-trends.

"Fierce has seen incredible results..." Interview with author, December 5, 2018, and further email correspondence.

"Dr. Zanette Johnson agrees..." Interview with author, October 3, 2017.

"*pseudo inefficacy*..." Daniel Västfjäll, Paul Slovic, and Marcus Mayorga, "Pseudoinefficacy: Negative Feelings from Children Who Cannot Be Helped Reduce Warm Glow for Children Who Can Be Helped," *Frontiers in Psychology* (May 18, 2015), ncbi.nlm.nih.gov/pmc/ articles/PMC4434905/.

"Slovic's work has shown..." Brian Resnick, "A Psychologist Explains the Limits of Human Compassion," Vox.com (July 19, 2017), vox.com/explainers/2017/7/19/15925506/psychic-numbing-paul-slovic-apathy.

"Psychologist Susan Spinrad Esterly..." Interview with author, March 6, 2018.

"Slovic talks about this idea of creating processes..." Brian Resnick, "A Psychologist Explains the Limits of Human Compassion," Vox.com (July 19, 2017), vox.com/explainers/2017/7/19/15925506/ psychic-numbing-paul-slovic-apathy.

Chapter 2: The Business Advantages of Empathy

"Nadella understands that empathy..." "Microsoft CEO Satya Nadella: How Empathy Sparks Innovation," Knowledge@Wharton website (February 22, 2018), knowledge.wharton.upenn.edu/article/ microsofts-ceo-on-how-empathy-sparks-innovation/.

"Project Aristotle revealed that..." Valerie Strauss, "The Surprising Thing Google Learned about Its Employees—and What It Means for Today's Students," *The Washington Post* (December 20, 2017),

washingtonpost.com/news/answer-sheet/wp/2017/12/20/the-
surprising-thing-google-learned-about-its-employees-and-what-
it-means-for-todays-students.

"The company empathized with both..." Jeff Booth, "Why Genuine
Empathy Is Good for Business," FastCompany.com (October 19,
2015), fastcompany.com/3052337/why-genuine-empathy-is-good-
for-business.

"'A critical lesson I learned at Apple..." Interview with author,
February 15, 2018.

"Surprised but intrigued, Google hired..." Valerie Strauss, "The
Surprising Thing Google Learned about Its Employees—and What
It Means for Today's Students," *The Washington Post* (December 20,
2017), washingtonpost.com/news/answer-sheet/wp/2017/12/20/
the-surprising-thing-google-learned-about-its-employees-and-
what-it-means-for-todays-students.

"2015 Deloitte leadership study..." Christie Smith and Stephanie
Turner, "The Radical Transformation of Diversity and Inclusion:
The Millennial Influence," Deloitte University Leadership Center
for Inclusion, www2.deloitte.com/content/dam/Deloitte/us/
Documents/about-deloitte/us-inclus-millennial-influence-
120215.pdf.

"They expect *cognitive diversity*..." Ibid.

"that's good news for organizations..." Ibid.

"According to a World Economic Forum article..." Belinda Parmar,
"8 Ways to Lead with Empathy," World Economic Forum website,
weforum.org/agenda/2016/02/8-ways-to-lead-with-empathy.

"'The shift we are seeing is not slight..." Interview with author,
November 1, 2017. Supporting statistics from: Amy Adkins,
"Millennials: The Job-Hopping Generation," Gallup: Workplace
(May 12, 2016), news.gallup.com/businessjournal/191459/
millennials-job-hopping-generation.aspx.

"According to Erica Dhawan, the leading authority..." Interview with
author, March 14, 2019.

"Studies by the Smith School of Business at Queen's University and
Gallup..." Emma Seppala and Kim Cameron, "Proof That Positive
Work Cultures Are More Productive," *Harvard Business Review*
(December 1, 2015), hbr.org/2015/12/proof-that-positive-work-
cultures-are-more-productive.

"Millennials demand a customer-centric..." Christopher Donnelly and
Renato Scaff, "Who Are the Millennial Shoppers? And What Do
They *Really* Want?" Accenture: Outlook, accenture.com/us-en/

insight-outlook-who-are-millennial-shoppers-what-do-they-really-
   want-retail.
"Gen Z 'never knew…'" "It's Lit: A Guide to What Teens Think Is Cool,"
   Google Cool Book, storage.googleapis.com/think/docs/its-lit.pdf.
"In fact, Brighton Jones has…" Melissa Crowe, "Washington State's
   Largest Wealth Management Firms," *Puget Sound Business
   Journal* (April 20, 2018), bizjournals.com/seattle/subscriber-
   only/2018/04/20/washington-states-largest-wealth.html.
"'The best any of us can do…'" Interview with author, March 13, 2018.

Chapter 3: The Empathy Veneer

"Each year, it publishes a list…" Belinda Parmar, "The Most Empathetic
   Companies, 2016," *Harvard Business Review* (December 1, 2016),
   hbr.org/2016/12/the-most-and-least-empathetic-companies-2016.
"'When we go in on day one…'" Interview with author, October 10, 2017.
"in 2017, a paying customer…" Scott Neuman, "Officers Fired after
   Forcible Removal of United Airlines Passenger," *The Two Way*,
   NPR (October 18, 2017), npr.org/sections/thetwo-way/2017/
   10/18/558469185/officers-fired-after-forcible-removal-of-
   united-airlines-passenger.
"its Transfarency® philosophy…" Southwest, southwest.com/html/air/
   transfarency/.
"Dave Ballai is chief information officer…" Interview with author,
   March 13, 2018.

Chapter 4: Benefits of Empathetic Leaders

"'I started traveling and meeting…'" Interview with author, June 12, 2017.
"According to the World Health Organization…" World Health
   Organization, "WHO Multi-country Study on Women's Health
   and Domestic Violence against Women," (2005), who.int/gender/
   violence/who_multicountry_study/fact_sheets/Peru2.pdf.
"'In any role, your success…'" Interview with author, March 13, 2018.
"Renee Metty is the founder of With Pause…" Interview with author,
   February 20, 2018.

"In a powerful *Forbes* article, he writes..." Jayson Boyers, "Why Empathy Is the Force That Moves Business Forward," Forbes.com (May 30, 2013), forbes.com/sites/ashoka/2013/05/30/why-empathy-is-the-force-that-moves-business-forward/#55497a0e169e.

"'Business success depends on empathetic leaders..." Ibid.

"'I saw that people in the financial industry..." Interview with author, April 17, 2018.

Chapter 5: Habits and Traits of Empathetic Leaders

"Paul Bloom, author of *Against Empathy*, believes that 'empathy is..." Paul Bloom, *Against Empathy: The Case for Rational Compassion* (Ecco, 2016).

"'What I've observed in working with leaders..." Interview with author, January 19, 2018.

"'When working to solve a complex operational problem..." Interview with author, September 15, 2017, and further correspondence.

"When she got back to Mexico..." Interview with author, June 20, 2017.

"Tibetan Buddhist nun and teacher Pema Chödrön..." Pema Chödrön, *When Things Fall Apart: Heart Advice for Difficult Times* (Shambhala Publications, anniversary edition, 2016).

"According to Chödrön..." Ibid.

"doing hard, challenging things..." Frances Bridges, "10 Ways to Build Confidence," Forbes.com (July 21, 2017), forbes.com/sites/frances-bridges/2017/07/21/10-ways-to-build-confidence/#7851d3363c59.

"She coaches her clients on this..." Interview with author, January 11, 2019.

"Andrew Marks is cofounder of SuccessHACKER..." Interview with author, November 27, 2017.

"Entrepreneur and yoga teacher Anna Guest-Jelley..." Interview with author, August 24, 2017.

"Linda J. Popky, founder of Leverage2Market Associates..." Correspondence with author, January 2019.

Chapter 6: Benefits of Empathetic Cultures

"'What's interesting and compelling about that..." Interview with author, February 27, 2018.

"According to the 2018 State of Workplace Empathy study..."
     Businessolver, "2018 State of Workplace Empathy Report," busi-
     nessolver.com/resources/state-of-workplace-empathy. The 2018
     study was taken by 1,850 U.S. employees, HR professionals, and
     CEOs within six industry sectors: education, healthcare, technology,
     manufacturing, financial services, and government. Specifically,
     1,000 employees, 100 HR professionals, 150 CEOs,
     and 600 industry professionals (100 per industry).
"Belinda Parmar of The Empathy Business writes..." Belinda
     Parmar, "The Most Empathetic Companies, 2016," *Harvard
     Business Review* (December 1, 2016), hbr.org/2016/12/
     the-most-and-least-empathetic-companies-2016.
"'CEOs overwhelmingly link financial performance...'" Businessolver,
     "Executive Summary: 2018 State of Workplace Empathy Study,"
     info.businessolver.com/empathy-2018-executive-summary-ty.
"a more empathetic, engaged workforce..." Jim Harter and Annamarie
     Mann, "The Right Culture: Not Just about Employee Satisfaction,"
     Gallup: Workplace (April 12, 2017), gallup.com/workplace/236366/
     right-culture-not-employee-satisfaction.aspx.
"One study shows that doctors who..." "Empathy May Reduce
     Malpractice Suits," JournalFeed abstract of D.D. Smith, J. Kellar,
     E.L. Walters, et al., "Does Emergency Physician Empathy Reduce
     Thoughts of Litigation? A Randomised Trial," *Emergency Medicine
     Journal* (August 2016), journalfeed.org/article-a-day/2016/
     empathy-may-reduce-malpractice-suits

Chapter 7: Habits and Traits of Empathetic Cultures

"Belinda suggested they switch..." Stephanie Newman, "Meet the
     CEO Embedding Empathy in Businesses across the Globe,"
     Writing on Glass (December 10, 2017), writingonglass.com/
     content/belinda-parmar-empathy-business.
"In some instances, this is actually required..." United States
     Breastfeeding Committee, "Workplace Support in Federal Law,"
     USBreastFeeding.org, usbreastfeeding.org/workplace-law.
"three stages to make these conversations..." Correspondence with
     author, March 18, 2019.
"Michelle Tillis Lederman, leadership speaker..." Correspondence
     with author, March 20, 2019.
"Dawson believes that Peace First's..." Interview with author,
     August 1, 2017.

"Jay Baer runs a remote organization, Convince & Convert..."
Interview with author, August 25, 2017.

"An employee from Nomo FOMO..." YEC Women, "Nine Ways to Boost
Company Culture with Remote Workers," Forbes.com (August 21,
2018), forbes.com/sites/yec/2018/08/21/nine-ways-to-boost-
company-culture-with-remote-workers/#4b8a630c6cd7.

"the driving factors for job satisfaction..." Jim Clifton, "Millennials: How
They Live and Work," Gallup: News (May 11, 2016), news.gallup
.com/opinion/chairman/191426/millennials-live-work.aspx.

"They issue an annual Avengers Award..." Next Jump, nextjump.com/
avengers2018/.

Chapter 8: Benefits of Empathetic Brands

"As senior technology leader Dave Ballai puts it..." Interview with author,
March 13, 2018.

"The process aims to capture..." "User Centered Design," Interaction
Design Foundation, interaction-design.org/literature/topics/
user-centered-design.

"With empathy imbued in your messaging..." Steve Olenski,
"Sustaining a Company through and beyond the Noise," Forbes
.com (October 4, 2016), forbes.com/sites/steveolenski/2016/10/
04/sustaining-a-company-through-and-beyond-the-noise-how-to-
develop-brand-longevity/#2b35b1be61ca.

"and true, according to Nordstrom spokespeople..." Christian Conte,
"Nordstrom Customer Service Tales Not Just Legend," Jacksonville
Business Journal (September 7, 2012), bizjournals.com/jacksonville/
blog/retail_radar/2012/09/nordstrom-tales-of-legendary-customer
.html.

"Round Table Companies founder and CEO Corey Blake..." Interview
with author, July 20, 2017.

"'If you're not focused on the customer..." "JetBlue: Inspiring Humanity
in Travel," *Outside In with Charles Trevail* (September 27, 2017),
cspace.com/podcast/jetblue-inspiring-humanity-in-travel/.

"As reported by Reuters..." Kyle Peterson and John Crawley, "JetBlue
Seen Able to Recover Image, Shares Rise," Reuters (February 21,
2007), reuters.com/article/jetblue-delays/jetblue-seen-able-to-
recover-image-shares-rise-idUSN2132721420070221.

"The authors note, 'In the zeal...'" Jay Baer and Daniel Lemin, *Talk Triggers: The Complete Guide to Creating Customers with Word of Mouth* (Portfolio, 2018).

"The company employs hundreds of refugees..." "Greek Yogurt Billionaire Fills His Plants with Refugees," CNN Business, YouTube video (September 21, 2015), youtube.com/watch?v=44rA8zME8mo.

"*Fast Company* had this to say..." Rob Brunner, "How Chobani's Hamdi Ulukaya Is Winning America's Culture War," *Fast Company* (March 20, 2017), fastcompany.com/3068681/how-chobani-founder-hamdi-ulukaya-is-winning-americas-culture-war.

Chapter 9: Habits and Traits of Empathetic Brands

"The company's original mission was..." "JetBlue: Inspiring Humanity in Travel," *Outside In with Charles Trevail* (September 27, 2017), cspace.com/podcast/jetblue-inspiring-humanity-in-travel/.

"According to REI's executive vice-president..." Kurt Schlosser, "REI Closing to #OptOutside Again on Black Friday while Pledging $1M to Study Benefits of Outdoors," GeekWire (October 23, 2018), geekwire.com/2018/rei-closing-optoutside-black-friday-pledging-1m-study-benefits-outdoors/.

"'We had a pure intent...'" Interview with author, January 17, 2019.

"REI was ranked the top CQ brand..." Charles Trevail, Manila Austin, Julie Wittes Schlack, and Katrina Lerman, "The Brands That Make Customers Feel Respected," *Harvard Business Review* (November 1, 2016), hbr.org/2016/11/the-brands-that-make-customers-feel-respected.

"the co-op itself reported..." REI Co-op, "REI Releases 2015 Stewardship and Earnings Report, Gives Back Three-Quarters of Profit to Outdoor Community and Opens Voting for Board Members," REI.com (March 15, 2016), newsroom.rei.com/news/rei-releases-2015-stewardship-and-earnings-report-gives-back-three-quarters-profit-to-outdoor-community-and-opens-voting-for-board-members.htm.

"Steele reports that this bold move..." Kurt Schlosser, "REI Closing to #OptOutside Again on Black Friday while Pledging $1M to Study Benefits of Outdoors," GeekWire (October 23, 2018), geekwire.com/2018/rei-closing-optoutside-black-friday-pledging-1m-study-benefits-outdoors/.

"As C Space so eloquently puts it..." Charles Trevail, Manila Austin, Julie Wittes Schlack, and Katrina Lerman, "The Brands That Make Customers Feel Respected," *Harvard Business Review* (November 1, 2016), hbr.org/2016/11/the-brands-that-make-customers-feel-respected.

"Marketing and customer service consultant Jay Baer..." Interview with author, August 25, 2017.

"'It began as a conversation,' says Daniel Rowan..." Interview with author, December 7, 2018.

"That was Southwest Airlines founder..." Shep Hyken, "How Happy Employees Make Happy Customers," Forbes.com (May 27, 2017), forbes.com/sites/shephyken/2017/05/27/how-happy-employees-make-happy-customers/#6545e2415c35.

"companies who master employee engagement..." Temkin Group, "2018 Temkin Experience Ratings (U.S.)" (March 2018), temkingroup.com/product/2018-temkin-experience-ratings-u-s/.

"As Mycoskie puts it..." Shana Lebowitz, "On the 10th Anniversary of TOMS, Its Founder Talks Stepping Down, Bringing in Private Equity, and Why Giving Away Shoes Provides a Competitive Advantage," *Business Insider* (June 15, 2016), businessinsider.com/toms-blake-mycoskie-talks-growing-a-business-while-balancing-profit-with-purpose-2016-6.

"United by Blue..." United by Blue, unitedbyblue.com/pages/our-mission.

"Mycoskie believes all this giving..." Shana Lebowitz, "On the 10th Anniversary of TOMS, Its Founder Talks Stepping Down, Bringing in Private Equity, and Why Giving Away Shoes Provides a Competitive Advantage," *Business Insider* (June 15, 2016), businessinsider.com/toms-blake-mycoskie-talks-growing-a-business-while-balancing-profit-with-purpose-2016-6.

"Marc Benioff—its founder, chairman, and CEO..." Dan Pontefract, "Salesforce CEO Marc Benioff Says the Business of Business Is Improving the State of the World," Forbes.com (January 7, 2017), forbes.com/sites/danpontefract/2017/01/07/salesforce-ceo-marc-benioff-says-the-business-of-business-is-improving-the-state-of-the-world/#7a95d8547eb0.

"Salesforce employees have donated..." Correspondence received from company representative, April 1, 2019.

"the company exceeds $13 billion..." Ibid.

"it launched its Sustainable Living Plan..." Unilever, unilever.com/sustainable-living.

"Since the initiative launched..." Unilever, "Unilever's Sustainable
   Living Plan Continues to Fuel Growth," press release (October 5,
   2018), unilever.com/news/press-releases/2018/unilevers-
   sustainable-living-plan-continues-to-fuel-growth.html.
"It also claims that it is on track..." Ibid.
"a 2017 *Forbes* article stated that..." Dan Pontefract, "Salesforce CEO
   Marc Benioff Says the Business of Business Is Improving the State
   of the World," Forbes.com (January 7, 2017), forbes.com/sites/
   danpontefract/2017/01/07/salesforce-ceo-marc-benioff-says-
   the-business-of-business-is-improving-the-state-of-the-world/
   #7a95d8547eb0.
"That headline generated a 400 percent increase..." Benyamin Elias,
   "The Secret to Writing Great Marketing Copy Is Market Research,"
   ActiveCampaign (March 19, 2018), activecampaign.com/blog/
   market-research-for-marketing-copy.
"Copywriter Joel Klettke..." Unbounce, "Joel Klettke—Unbounce Call
   to Action Conference 2017 #ctaconf," YouTube video (July 10,
   2017), youtube.com/watch?v=bsY2rbzukH0.
"'I've rented a cabin in Denver..." Maria Ross, *Branding Basics for
   Small Business: How to Create an Irresistible Brand on Any Budget*
   (NorLights Press, 2nd Edition, 2014).

Conclusion

"These experiences inspired her..." Neda Nobari Foundation,
   nnf.foundation/west-of-middle-east.
"Empathetic leaders cultivate loyalty..." Victor Lipman, "How Important
   Is Empathy to Successful Management?" Forbes.com (February 24,
   2018), forbes.com/sites/victorlipman/2018/02/24/how-important-
   is-empathy-to-successful-management/#cc68c1ca46d7.

ABOUT THE AUTHOR

MARIA ROSS is the founder of Red Slice, a consultancy that advises entrepreneurs, startups, and fast-growth businesses on how to build an irresistible brand story and authentically connect with customers. She is a keynote speaker who regularly speaks to audiences on marketing and building an engaging brand story that drives growth and impact. She is the author of *Branding Basics for Small Business* and the Juicy Guides ebook series for entrepreneurs.

Maria started her career as a management consultant with Accenture and went on to build marketing and brand strategies for multiple companies, including Discovery Communications, Monster.com, BusinessObjects (now SAP), and many other startups and technology leaders, before starting her own business. As a brand strategist, she has worked with brands such as Microsoft, Dropbox, Alteryx, and GSK, as well as many smaller leaders in niche industries. Maria has been featured in and written for numerous media outlets, including MSNBC, *Entrepreneur* magazine, *Huffington Post*, and Forbes.com.

Maria understands the power of empathy at both a brand and personal level: in 2008, six months after launching her business, she suffered a ruptured brain aneurysm that almost killed her. Her humorous and heartfelt memoir about surviving this health crisis, *Rebooting My Brain*, has received worldwide praise.

Maria lives with her husband, young son, and precocious black lab mutt in the San Francisco Bay Area.

www.red-slice.com
www.theempathyedge.com

Continue the Empathy Conversation

- **COPIES FOR YOUR TEAM, CUSTOMERS, CLIENTS, OR ORGANIZATION:** Want to spread the power of empathy within your organization or share these tips with your clients? Please let me know if I can help with a speaking event or multiple book sales, and I will be glad to assist. Contact me at empathy@red-slice.com.

- **REVIEW:** If you enjoyed *The Empathy Edge*, I'd appreciate if you left a review online with your preferred retailer. Reviews help readers find my book, which will spread the word about the business benefits of empathy. Thank you for being part of the empathy revolution by leaving a review to help spread the word!

- **NEWSLETTER:** Join the thousands of other empathy enthusiasts by signing up for my weekly newsletter. Enjoy insights on how to cultivate your empathy and boost your brand's impact and visibility. Be kind, pass it on. Sign up at www.theempathyedge.com.

- **CONNECT ON SOCIAL MEDIA:** Empathy is alive and well and living online. Connect with me in the following places and let's build an Empathy Army (#EmpathyEdge).

www.red-slice.com
www.theempathyedge.com
Twitter @redslice
Instagram @redslicemaria
LinkedIn www.linkedin.com/in/mariajross/